COLLATERAL DAMAGE

COLLATERAL DAMAGE

**The impacts of
my mother's
mental illness
on me**

CATE GRACE

ISBN: 978-1523851799

Printed in the United States of America

Book design by Jean Boles
jean.bolesbooks@gmail.com

Book cover art by Stefanie Bennet
Instagram: stefbennett.art.

This book is dedicated to all children of parental mental illness—including the grown-up ones.

The events in this book are portrayed to the best of my memory. Names and identifying details have been changed to protect the privacy of the people involved. Exact dialogue has been reconstructed to the best of my recollection.

– Cate Grace

They say
it takes a village to raise a child.
I say
sometimes the village,
though well-intentioned,
misses the mark.

AUTHOR'S NOTE

When I began writing my story, my siblings were horrified that I would disclose this information. They said that they did not want people knowing what was, in effect, their story, too.

I understand their reaction, their fear.

This is a story about mental illness. Mental illness is stigmatizing. As co-inhabitants of a household where mental illness lived, as children growing up together—surviving together—in a highly dysfunctional household, it is difficult to respect their privacy, to honor the keeping of their story, in the telling of mine. My story blurs into theirs. No wonder my siblings were upset.

One sister suggested that I write this under a pen name. I worry that hiding behind a pen name makes me feel as though I am too ashamed to stand up and say, "This is what happened to me." Hiding my identity seems to support the stigma attached to mental illness, which I do not want to do.

CATE GRACE

I share my story in the hopes that people will begin to understand what it is like for a child to grow up in a household dominated by mental illness. I hope that others who grew up like me will not feel so alone, will recognize the scars they carry, the wounding they constantly need to acknowledge and address.

I hope that the telling of this story will help policy makers and service providers address the collateral damage, particularly to children, of mental illness in families.

Telling my story is also part of my way in moving forward with my own healing.

Each of my family members has a right to their own way forward, which may or may not involve them ever telling their story.

In honoring my intentions for memorializing what happened to me for others to read, there is no need to disclose the identities of my sisters, my brother, my father, and my mother. Each has their own perspective of our shared history. Each has a right to their privacy.

Each has endured enough of their own pain, their own shame, their own loss of self-worth and broken dreams.

I cannot, and will not, add to that.

So I have changed the names of my family members. And I have changed mine. This protects their individual healing processes while allowing my healing to continue.

I love them, and I respect their privacy.

This isn't their story. It's mine.

Abandoned

She stays there, in the corner
Little girl lost, thrown away, not good enough
Discarded.

As real as the air I breathe.
As much a part of me as my fingers.

I keep her away from me
Around her—this core of me
I have constructed walls spun from confidence, a sense of
belonging
Not raw materials, but manufactured.

Not to keep her away from me.
But to keep me away from her.

She dictates that I will always be, at most
A happy-sad person.
But I am content with that.

Two steps forward; one step back
Sometimes one step forward and two steps back.

Half truths around which I spin my speculation
Malevolent motivations dressed in counterfeit clothes.
Lost. Thrown away. Not good enough.
So begins the erosion of my sense of myself.

The walls, so carefully constructed, not so sturdy after all.
Cracks appear, then gaping holes.

The dust of my confidence settles around the wreckage.
And there she is.
And there I am.

CHAPTER ONE

The baby's wails grew louder, more desperate. From the living room where the little boy had been quietly playing with blocks as his mother slept on the couch, the screaming was an insistent noise, with periods of crescendo followed by brief intervals of silence.

The little boy knew that his mother wanted him to be quiet. Woken from her stupor, she had already yelled at him and slapped him when he had built his blocks up into a tower as tall as he was, and then, loud tractor noises emanating from him as he, both creator and destroyer, gleefully knocked the tower to the ground. He knew the baby needed to be quiet or his mother would lash out at him again—or at the baby. He had experienced both and wanted neither.

His father, a farmer from a line of farmers stretching back as far as the family history reached, was usually gone from early in the morning until late afternoon. If he was able to pick up contracting work with his big yellow bulldozer, he was sometimes gone even longer. The only exception was

Sunday morning, which always meant breakfast and church together as a family. If his mother was too tired on Sunday morning, his dad cooked breakfast, and the little boy loved helping his dad make breakfast. His dad would joke with the little boy, tell him stories, and show him how to make crispy bacon and perfect scrambled eggs. The little boy's job was to make the toast, which he did carefully, his tongue poking out of his mouth as he concentrated, his little arm and hand not always accurate or coordinated. Even if the toast burned or the butter went on in big, uneven blobs, the little boy's dad praised him and told him that he was the best toast-maker in the county.

The little boy couldn't wait to be a farmer, a contractor, a man—just like his dad.

The toddler tugged on his sleeping mother's pajama sleeve again. Her only response was to grunt and violently push him away, and then turn onto her side.

The toddler went to the baby's room, as he had been doing for the past several hours. Throughout the morning and into the afternoon, through the din of the crying and screaming, their mother continued to lie on the couch.

The little boy went to the crib in the darkened room, the bright light of midday shut out by heavy curtains.

"Hi, baby Cate, don't cry," he crooned to her as he petted her sweating head. Her crying made him have a tummy ache. He did not know how to stop the crying.

The little boy wrinkled his nose; the baby stunk like poopy wet diapers—as she did nearly every day until his daddy came in after a day of farm work and cleaned her. He had

14

seen the baby's fiery red bottom when his daddy cleaned her, and his father had not responded when he asked whether little girls had red bottoms while little boys had white ones. His happy-go-lucky father used to whistle and hum when he came in from working outside and always spent time talking to his son. Since the baby arrived his father was often silent.

Not yet three years old, the little boy knew that his mother could not take care of this baby. He was a big boy; he could take care of himself, and he was proud that he was able to find food in the cupboard to eat. But this baby was always crying, and the little boy had tried to share with her the crackers and donuts he found to eat, but she had refused them.

The little boy remembered that there were several half-used bottles of formula in the kitchen sink, piled up from the previous few days. The baby liked to drink out of the bottles and sometimes stopped crying when she drank. Maybe she was thirsty, he reasoned. Maybe that would stop her crying.

He made his way to the kitchen and pushed a chair up to the sink. With some effort, he climbed up, his chubby little legs flailing as he pulled himself up on the seat of the chair onto his belly, and then carefully straightened up to stand. He fished a bottle from the dirty dishes in the dishpan, climbed down off the chair, and went back to the wailing baby.

The bottle barely fit through the slats in the crib, and the little boy's small arm was just able to reach the baby. His first several attempts to find her mouth missed, and the baby cried even harder, her toothless mouth wide open to show her tongue, vibrating with her screams. The little boy's tummy ache worsened. Finally, he was able to keep the nipple of the bottle poised over her mouth, and the baby latched onto the bottle, continuing to moan while she desperately sucked the half-empty bottle.

I was this baby.

I am Cate.

As a tiny baby
I knew
in the deepest part of my heart:
I am on my own.
And that knowledge
made me feel
even smaller.

CHAPTER TWO

My father says that I cried for the first two years of my life. My response to him was always that I cried because I knew what was coming, which caused us both to laugh. In the few photos I have of myself from those very early years, I see a frail little body and enormous dark eyes framed by a tiny pinched face. Never am I smiling or laughing.

For many years I would look at those pictures and wonder, what was happening with that tiny me?

When I was two years old, I was diagnosed with failure to thrive. I always assumed it simply meant that I did not gain weight properly. My sister Joan, born 13 months after me, was always my size or taller, and people often assumed we were either twins or that she was older than me. People would tease me and call me the runt of the family.

But that diagnosis is so much more than not growing, goes so much deeper than the physical effects of inadequate nutrition. That diagnosis is one of the first indications of the impact of my mother's severe mental illness on me. I did not grow or develop well. I did not prosper or flourish. I did not *thrive*.

I understand now that the impacts of my mother's mental illness began to manifest in me when I was born.

Babies are completely and utterly helpless. The baby must rely upon those around her to survive. Each and every need of the infant is communicated through crying: if the infant is hungry, the infant cries; if the infant is cold, the infant cries; if the infant is wet, or dirty, or uncomfortable, or frightened, the infant cries. If no one comes, or if the cries are met with a response only from time to time, eventually the infant stops crying. And the infant begins to believe, based upon her experience thus far with life, that her needs will not be met by anyone outside herself.

This belief, coupled with her helplessness, is a form of depression. She stops eating, she stops crying, she loses interest in a life she is not certain she will ever survive long enough to ever fully participate in.

That's what happened to me.

Not because my mother was evil, but because my mother was desperately mentally ill.

The first notes of the song of myself
—the building blocks of the me yet to be—
Were the harsh grating cries of my solo,
The noisy din of my fight to survive.

That song
can never be
unsung.

CHAPTER THREE

I sit in the very back row of the crowded little room, ready to take notes to report back to my boss. A ladylike woman, determined and passionate about mental health issues, my boss is a state policymaker, driven by a profound desire to make a difference in a system she knew was broken, but a system she believed could, and should, be fixed. She knew nothing about my story, could not know that I had, at best, a lukewarm enthusiasm for the subject, that as a result of my childhood I avoided mentally ill people and the issues of mental illness whenever I could.

It is a beautiful West Australian late spring morning. I would so much rather be doing anything else—even sitting in my office doing research—than attending this meeting. I am uncomfortable with the feelings this gathering stirs in me.

I am at a meeting organized by three mental health advocates, women who are interested in forming a new group to advocate for children living with a parent or parents with mental health issues. We are meeting in the

CATE GRACE

back room of a mental health non-profit, non-government organization. Mismatched chairs are lined up in the room, and an urn of hot water and jars of coffee, tea, sugar and milk are on a table right outside the door. There is a jumble of chipped, stained cups, so often the hallmark of earnest, passionate, underfunded, overworked organizations such as this, waiting to be used by the attendees.

The meeting was widely advertised in the community, and I am astonished at the demographic of attendees, many of whom are in their forties and fifties. Most surprising to me is the number of men in the room—nearly half the attendees—as I expected this subject would equate to a "soft" social issue, and therefore of greater interest to women.

I am also surprised at the number of attendees, and it is obvious that the three organizers are also shocked. As more and more people pour into the room, eventually there is standing room only. Still more people continue to crowd in, and many of us put our chairs outside the room and stand so that more people can squeeze into the room. I look around the room for the usual public servants and non-profit officers who attend such meetings, and I realize that most of the attendees appear to be members of the community.

The mood in the room is somber and apprehensive. Generally, such meetings provoke small talk, even amongst strangers, but there is a strange quiet in the room, and the few people who talk do so in whispers. Nobody makes eye contact and everyone seems uncomfortable. Yet no one leaves, and people continue to crowd into the small room.

Though I am here in my professional capacity, I suddenly realize that I belong here in my own personal right. It is a shock when it dawns on me that many of the people in this room had a very similar childhood to mine. It is only then that I, too, avoid eye contact and feel uncomfortable.

The women finally get started. They are nervous, and stumble when explaining the purpose of this meeting and their vision for recognizing and addressing the discrete effects of parental mental illness on children. They tell us a bit about themselves. They, too, are adult children of a mentally ill parent. We are all bonded by our common childhood. We collectively understand their unease, and I feel the room relaxing. Every person with this childhood understands how difficult it must be for these three brave women to form this group, to tell us their story, to volunteer to lead the way to acknowledging the effects of our shared childhood.

We all understand how difficult it is to break the secrecy that necessarily envelopes a childhood like ours.

They finally turn off the lights and show a short video done by an advocacy group in a different state.

The video has clips of adults talking about growing up in a household dominated by parental mental illness, interspersed with children talking about life with their mentally ill parent. Each segment strikes raw pain and deep understanding within me, and I can feel the lump in my throat growing. I struggle to hold back my tears. At the beginning and the end of the video a group of mental health advocates earnestly appeals to policymakers and the community to be aware of this issue, and suggests ways to provide support to children living with a mentally ill parent. The group urges awareness and support for the adult children of parental mental health issues, too, pointing out that the detrimental effects of this type of childhood often need addressing no matter the age of the "child."

When the video ends and the lights come back on, many of the men are wiping their eyes and blowing their nose. Most of the women, including me and the three organizers, are quietly weeping.

Nobody speaks for several minutes.

It is apparent that this little meeting, this little video, has struck a raw nerve. I glance around the room at all these people and my heart aches for us collectively.

For the first time in my life I am consciously aware of the collateral damage caused by severe mental illness on family members. It is also the first time that I realize that I am not alone in my childhood, and my sense of kinship with these weeping strangers causes me to struggle even harder to not cry. That awareness provokes a rush of powerful emotions in me, feelings I had long repressed.

And like a shiny new key turning in a rusted lock, the painful childhood I had so carefully packed away tumbles into my reality.

Brave truth
inspires
more brave truth.
Be
brave truth.

CHAPTER FOUR

Human beings are naturally very inquisitive, which has led to all kinds of wonderful inventions and improvements in the way we live. But when you have the childhood I had, that curiosity required me to have a story ready for the inevitable questions about my family and my parents.

As a young adult I described my mother by putting my pointer finger to the side of my head, making large circles with my finger, rolling my eyes, and saying that she was crazy. "No," I would insist when the reaction was hesitant laughter. "She really is."

And then I would stop, knowing that an explanation beyond that was simply a waste of time. The resulting awkward silence would pass because I would quickly make a joke about something less personal. I became adept at smoothly, rapidly changing the subject and making people feel more comfortable.

That was my prepared description of my mother. That description evolved throughout my twenties. I found that saying less led to more questions. Saying more led to all sorts of things, none of which I was ready or willing to deal with.

By the time I was thirty, with a demanding career, a daughter of my own, and a short, failing marriage to contend with, I had put the first part of my life away in a large, dusty trunk in my mind, locked up securely. I had no intention of ever opening it back up to sift through its contents. I wanted to forget my childhood and move on with my life.

But our childhood has an enormous impact on who we are and how we journey through the rest of our life. This is true whether we want it to be or not. Forgetting about my childhood or pretending it did not happen would never negate its impact on my adult life.

It is a fact that as an adult I carry the effects of my childhood with me. The insidious damage caused by the mental illness that invaded my childhood home and resided in my mother continues to impact my life in all sorts of ways.

More facts:

✓ Mental illness covers a variety of diagnoses.

✓ Most mentally ill people are not violent.

✓ Most mentally ill people are far more a threat to themselves than to anyone else.

✓ Many mentally ill people are able to function and lead productive lives, with varying degrees of support.

✓ Mental illness can be treated.

These facts are supported by a mountain of research and often cited to disprove some of the commonly held myths about mental illness.

And:

✓ Mentally ill people continue to be marginalized in western society.

✓ The stigma of being mentally ill continues to be disabling in its own right.

These are facts, too, backed up not only by research but by the media, social media, and common experience.

And finally:

✓ The effects of a person's mental illness are not confined to that person, but extend to their family and loved ones.

This is a fact, too. It is well known by those who have experienced it. It is rarely studied or acknowledged, and the extent of the effects are not very well understood— even by those who have experienced it.

Like all children of parents with mental illness I have a higher risk of developing mental illness than other children.[1] I am also at high risk for behavioral problems, major depression and anxiety disorders, and I was more

---

[1] The Royal Australian and New Zealand College of Psychiatrists Position Paper 56, October 2009 Children of Parents with a Mental Illness; The Effects of Parental Mental Illness on Children-Deep Blue, deepblue.lib.umich.edu/bitstream/handle/2027.42/.../lslomins_1/pdf; Facts for Families, American Academy of Child & Adolescent Psychiatry, issue 39, December 2008.

likely to suffer developmental delays, poorer school performance and peer issues. [2]

That my mother had children was not unusual, as many adults with a serious mental illness are parents of dependent children. [3]

This is my story, the story of a person who grew up with an unwelcome intruder firmly attached to her mother, and the effects of that intruder on me. It was only as an adult that I came to know the name and nature of that intruder and began to understand the enormity of the impact of that illness on myself and my family.

Though my mother's mental illness was most certainly unwelcome, it was no stranger. I came to know it well. I first knew mental illness because it resided inside my mother. Then mental illness found a home inside my sister. But that's not all that unusual, because mental illness also lived inside my mother's mother.

Many mental illnesses like to stay in the same family. My story, however, is not about me having conquered a mental illness in my own right. It is only partly about

---

[2] Rutter & Quinton, 1984; Beardslee, Gladstone, Wright & Cooper, 1998; Nomura, Wickramaratne, Warner, Mufson & Weissman, 2002; Sameroff & Seifer, 1983; Weintraub & Neal, 1984; Nomura et al, 2002, as reported by Michelle D Sherman, PhD, at http://www.socialworktoday.com/archive/septoct2007p26.shtml

[3] The Royal Australian and New Zealand College of Psychiatrists Position Paper 56, October 2009, Children of Parents with a Mental Illness, reports that 29-35% of mental health services clients are female parents of dependent children; statistics from the United States put that figure at 68%. Nicholson, Biebel, Katz-Leavy & Williams, 2004, as reported by Michelle D Sherman, PhD, at http://www.socialworktoday.com/archive/septoct2007p26.shtml

growing up without a mother. I carry with me the discrete and unique effects of growing up with a mother with severe mental illness, effects which I have only come to identify and understand with the passage of time. This story is about the effects of my mother's disease on me.

According to the United States Air Force Intelligence Targeting Guide, "collateral damage" is defined as:

[the] unintentional or incidental damage... occurring as a result of military actions directed against targeted enemy forces or facilities. Such damage can occur to friendly, neutral, and even enemy forces.

Collateral damage is the unintentional death, injury, or damage inflicted incidentally to an intended target.

My family sustained collateral damage. Mental illness targeted my mother, but the rest of us were incidentally damaged. Mental illness is not a heat-seeking missile, but a scatter bomb, spewing destruction and damage so that those closest to its target are inevitably harmed.

The collateral damage caused by my mother's illness occurred over many years. The damage was repeated over and over again, the effects stamped into deep grooves in our individual psyches. That kind of deeply reinforced, sustained damage resulted in responsive thought processes and behavioral patterns that the children of parents with a serious mental illness carry for the rest of their lives.

As a teenager and young adult I was not aware of the effects of my mother's mental illness on me. I did not know that so many aspects of my life directly reflected the collateral damage of my mother's severe mental illness. It was only as I grew older, had children of my own, was able to step back and away from my childhood and look at it as an adult that I started to recognize and understand the ongoing impacts of my childhood in my life. I also began to realize that I could not escape those impacts, that pretending away my childhood was not working.

Every child with a severely mentally ill parent will have their own version of that collateral damage, their unique adaptations to their childhood. I can only tell the story about the collateral damage mental illness caused in my situation.

I am grateful each and every day, as only the child of a person with severe mental illness can be, for having escaped the disease in my own right.

I have not experienced the agony of hearing voices no one else can hear, or the sense of being utterly convinced that my loved ones are trying to kill me. I cannot describe how that feels.

I have not experienced the helplessness and dependence wrought by being unable to hold down a job, or live on my own, or have a normal social life.

I can only imagine those things.

But I can tell you about the collateral damage, because I experienced it.

Damage
though unintentional
is still
damage.

CHAPTER FIVE

I am standing on a chair in front of the kitchen sink, helping my mother dry dishes. I am three years old and feel very grown up and so happy to be helping my mom. The breeze blows through the window in front of the sink, and I can hear the sounds of my life on this soft summer morning: birds singing, my five-year-old brother making muted noises of "Boom! Boom! Boom!" as he plays with his matchbox cars in the sand pile my dad made for him outside the open screen door; a tractor off in the distance; the sound of the water as my mother washes the dishes, my mother singing.

I like when my mother sings, because it means she is in a good mood. When my mother is in a good mood we are all in a good mood. When she is in a bad mood, everything is pretty bad.

She is often in a bad mood because she has all these kids to take care of and she never wanted any children. My father works the long hours of a farmer, so she is alone with us most of the day. My big brother is the best at staying out of her way and playing quietly. My baby sister used to cry, but she stays quiet now. Of the three of us, I am the one who is the most trouble to her because I cry a lot and I am small and unhealthy. I know all of this because she tells me.

I am careful as I handle each dish and use the driest parts of the dish towel to completely wipe each dish dry. My mother is critical and periodically checks to see that I have dried them completely. I want to do it right to please her, and I listen to her instructions to me carefully. I don't want to disappoint her or make her angry, and I am relieved when, satisfied with my work, she goes back to washing and singing.

But I also have to keep up with her because she will be angry if too many dishes stack up, so I am trying to be careful but fast. She washes dishes so much faster than I am able to carefully dry them. She is an expert at dish washing and I am a dish-drying novice. My stomach starts to hurt as the dishes begin to pile up, but I keep going, careful but fast, careful but fast, careful but fast.

Then I drop a bowl. It is a plastic bowl, so it does not break. It makes a loud crashing sound, then more little crashing sounds as it bounces across the floor several times before stopping to rest against the wall.

My mother's singing stops and she screams at me and shakes me. Her fingers are claws, digging into my shoulders as she shakes me hard. My shoulders hurt where the claws are biting, and my head jerks back and forth. My teeth rattle and I concentrate on not biting my tongue.

She screams at me that I am not even able to dry dishes properly. Her face has a large dark hole for a mouth, and two small dark holes for eyes.

I shrink back away from her.

I do not recognize her.

I am afraid of her.

My baby self could not recognize
Where I stop and you start
I am instinctively bound to you, part of you
We we we we we.

When I start to see myself separately from you
The intruder in our home screams at me
hurts me
tells me
I you I you I you I you I you!

Only then do I realize,
deep in my bones
that I am
completely inadequate
totally unworthy
utterly unlovable...
even to my own mother.

CHAPTER SIX

That one incident from my deepest memory best defines the relationship I had with my mother.

I was afraid of her.

And I desperately wanted to please her so she would love me.

My mother's transformation into a powerful, clawed, faceless monster capable of hurting me happened frequently. Sometimes the faceless monster did not physically hurt me, but said terrible things to me and about me, causing more damage than a punch in the nose or a beating. I did not know that it was the intruder in our home that caused this transformation; I assumed I was somehow responsible.

I have come to realize that when I dream about my mother, as I occasionally do, I am in great fear in my waking life. In those dreams my mother is not necessarily scary, or even in a starring role. That my mother continues to be my

CATE GRACE

subconscious symbol for terror could actually be funny if it weren't true.

Given this childhood a surprising positive emerged: there is very little I fear as an adult. Many things that other adults might find frightening pale in comparison to the constant fear I carried as a child.

The second defining aspect of my relationship with my mother is much more troubling. Even today, more than forty years later, as I sit in my house on a quiet Sunday morning, with the sun shining and a beautiful summer breeze blowing, a tiny part of me stubbornly continues to believe that if I had only been a "better" daughter, perhaps then my mother would have loved me. A small but stubborn part of me still whispers, "What if?"

I spent my childhood and much of my adulthood trying very hard to please the people around me, even at the expense of my own sense of myself. I reasoned that if only I was a better person, more competent, more skilled, more intelligent, faster, a better worker—the list goes on and on—then my mother would love me. And if my mother could love me, maybe others could love me, too.

This manifested in being an over-achiever, a workaholic, a straight-A student. I rarely said no when asked to go above and beyond, even when doing so harmed me. I had it all, but I kept driving myself to what I now realize was an impossible goal. No matter what I was able to accomplish, still I knew I was inadequate; still my mother could not love me. On the outside I looked driven, successful; on the inside I could not fill the empty parts of myself.

I have made progress. As I have grown older and worked on myself, the part of me that believes I was not loveable even to my own mother has gotten smaller. The part of me that believes I was to blame for her not loving me has diminished, too. But I have not rid myself of those beliefs entirely. Those beliefs are my default setting. All I can do is be aware of those beliefs, and in that awareness, try to counter their effects on my life.

When a friendship sours, I immediately assume it is my fault.

When someone tells me that I'm not good enough, I believe it to be true.

When a relationship ends, I have to fight the voice inside my head that berates me, telling me that the relationship ended because I am unlovable.

When I am not successful, I know it is because I don't deserve success.

When I am successful, I feel guilty, knowing I am not deserving.

When the one person in the world who was supposed to love me and care for me did not, that had a crucial Impact on my view of my own lovability. My view of myself has had an enormous effect on my relationships. At a very deep level I have gone through life believing I do not deserve love or happiness. As a young adult this often manifested in being happy to be with anyone who liked me or paid attention to me, irrespective of whether they were good for me or not.

I didn't know what I didn't know. I had no idea why I frequently had unhealthy relationships where I derived so little yet gave so much.

I remember exactly when I figured this out. My daughter Briana taught me.

When Briana was nine years old, her after-school care provider was waiting to speak with me one day. She told me that there had been some trouble with Briana that day. A boy told Briana that he liked her, and Briana and her friends decided that he wasn't "cool" enough. So she and her friends wrote a letter to the boy, outlining all the various reasons she didn't like him, including that he was ugly and stupid.

Thankfully, the care provider intercepted the letter. I was the angriest I have ever been with my daughter. I lectured her all the way home about how flattering and wonderful it is to have another human being open up their heart and take a chance on you, trusting you with their precious feelings. I told her she was a pretty girl, inside and out, and she had many years ahead of her of boys telling her they liked her, so she had better get used to being kind in her response.

At the end of that long, angry lecture, my gorgeous daughter looked at me through teary eyes and said, wailing, "But I don't like him, Mom!"

Her truthful reaction to the attentions of this boy, though lacking tact, taught me a valuable lesson. At the age of nine my daughter consciously knew what she wanted and needed, and she was not willing to settle for less. I hope and pray that she never falters from this. She knows she is special and wonderful and loved. That sense of herself will only allow her to look out for her own highest good. She will not "settle."

I am still learning how to do this.

What is the role that my mother plays in my life? What is the shape of my adult relationship with her? How do I forge the way forward in the wake of the massive collateral damage caused by mental illness in my mother?

For me, the way forward is beyond. I have painstakingly severed what was at best a tenuous connection to a woman with whom I have never had a healthy emotional bond. I have seen her only a few times, briefly, in the past thirty years. I do not know her at all, this woman who carried me within herself, gave birth to me and with whom I share 50% of my DNA and 100% of my first eighteen years of life.

On hands and knees, head bowed, I crawl to you
I so want you to love me.
I need you.

Screaming, terrified, I run away from you
I am so afraid of you!
And still I need you.

I breathe, eyes closed, the sword slashes
The complex knot between us gone.
Now a chasm where need used to live.

The intruder victorious.
No winners.
No prize.

CHAPTER SEVEN

I am eighteen years old. It is the day to move into the dormitory at the state university where I have been accepted on an honors scholarship. This is the jumping-off point to the next phase of my life. My car, packed with all my possessions, is waiting for me in the crowded church parking lot. I have been living with my friend and her family for the past six months, so my possessions have already been whittled down to a carload.

I have a detour to make before I head off to college.

I am in the church with hundreds of other people mourning the death of my sixteen-year-old friend Jeff, who paid the ultimate price of mixing alcohol and driving. I have known Jeff most of my life. A sweet, happy teenager with big blue eyes who always had a smile, Jeff could—and would—talk to anyone and was kind and inclusive.

I was at the bar with Jeff the night of his death; I even walked to his pickup with him and his friend to ride with them to the party they were so determined to attend. My brother, also in the bar, saw me leave with the two obviously drunk young men and came after me to convince me to stay at the bar. When I got the call at my waitressing job the next morning, tired and hung-over, I slumped to the floor, simultaneously overcome with grief and shock and thankful that I did not get into that truck with them.

Jeff is the first young person I have known to have died, and I am profoundly shaken by the knowledge that our youth does not make us invincible. I am deeply upset that Jeff's kindness and goodness did not keep him from dying before he ever had a chance to become the wonderful man he was sure to be.

I arrive at the church by myself, and though I am surrounded by people I know, I feel very alone.

When the service ends I drive myself the ninety miles to where I will be spending the next four years of my life. I know that this day will forever stand out in my mind, this day of new beginnings marked by such sadness.

When I get to the university town it is buzzing with the excitement of a new school year. The population of this small town doubles with the influx of 30,000 students every September, and the streets, shops, cafes, restaurants and public spaces are crowded. Cars are triple-parked in front of the dormitories, and everywhere I look I see nervous new students moving into the dorms, carrying suitcases and bean bag chairs and lamps and posters, flanked by parents and siblings.

I park my car in the only available spot several blocks from the dorm and carry my first load of possessions into the crowded lobby to get my room assignment and key. I am sweaty, tired and alone. Two student housing staff and the senior student resident advisor greet me enthusiastically, telling me to have my parents join me in the briefing they are about to provide to me about my new residence. Their bright smiles fade when I tell them it is just me. Undeterred, they launch excitedly into a well-rehearsed five-minute presentation about dorm rules and campus information, peppered with how much fun I am going to have. They finish by advising of several good restaurants where "we" can go to celebrate my move into the dorm, then flustered, awkwardly stop and force too-bright smiles when they remember that there is no family here to take me out to dinner.

I have no parents or siblings to help me. It appears to me as though I am the only person moving into the dorms with absolutely no help or support. I am embarrassed.

Thankfully, my two roommates have already moved in and are away with their families for dinner. I make several trips to retrieve my things, each time feeling more alone. I watch as parents hug their tearful children goodbye. I watch as many parents break down as soon as they are out of sight of their children.

As I lie in my bed in my new surroundings, the first night of this phase of my life, unable to sleep, I think about my friend Jeff, so deeply mourned by his parents and siblings and family and friends.

I think about how I moved into the dorms by myself.

I wonder if my parents and siblings even know where I am.

Or if they care.

No herd, no pack, no gaggle, no flock
An island of one
Surrounded by belonging
Claimed by none.

CHAPTER EIGHT

Lest you think I've led a secretive life, I have not. I have told this story, in bits and pieces, to numerous people as I've journeyed on the path of my life. I have loving friends who know my story. I've also told relative strangers parts of the story, when the story itself, eager to leave that dark dusty place in my mind, took over, insisting upon being told.

There are many people I have encountered in my life who I am sure have no idea of the effect they had on me. I met a priest once when I was seventeen, a wonderful man to whom I told parts of my story, who saw the parts of me that were broken. I met him at a weekend retreat and never saw him again, yet every year for many years I received a birthday greeting from that kind man, each with a different inspirational verse, each verse perfectly appropriate at the time.

Every person has people in their lives like Father Schmidt, people who in some large or small way have a lasting and important impact. I completely left the church a few years after that encounter, but religion didn't forge that bond between us. His humanity did. He reached out to me and assured me, year after year, that he remembered me and continued to care about me.

Sometimes the impact a person has on you is simply and solely knowing that they care.

Or maybe it's knowing that someone else in this great wide world knows what it is like to be you.

Has walked in your shoes. Lived inside your skin. Looked out through your eyes.

Comprehends the incomprehensible.

I spent the first four decades of my life feeling isolated in my childhood experiences, ashamed and embarrassed. As soon as we were able, we siblings, stark reminders of our childhood, avoided one another, contributing even more to my sense that I was alone.

Many of my adult friends, the products of healthy parent-child relationships, spent increasing amounts of time with their parents, siblings, and extended families as they grew older. My immediate family throughout my twenties was empty, and throughout my thirties and forties consisted of my father and occasionally an intermittent sibling.

I yearned to be part of a large, healthy family and to that end, I tried unsuccessfully to reunite my siblings, organizing family get-togethers, calling, writing, trying to keep in touch to develop and maintain a connection with people who had no desire to see or talk to me, nor to one another. My brother's wife, on my brother's instruction, always told me he was not home when I called to talk to him—even when he was sitting next to the phone. My sisters often ignored my advances and invitations, or responded with apathy, or—worse yet—anger. Always, I was the laboring oar, and the consistent lack of response or half-hearted responses were painful and contributed to my sense that I bore some responsibility for our childhood.

It also made me feel even more isolated and alone.

I was struggling to move our relationships forward under the assumption that we could forget—and had forgotten—the very thing that linked us in the first place: our childhood.

We children had no control over what happened in our childhood home. In that context our adult responses to behaving as a family make perfect sense: we asserted control.

Sometimes children who grew up with a severely mentally ill parent may respond as I did and try to "fix" things to achieve a healthy family many years after the fact. That was my way to assert control. I did not realize that I could not fix our broken family, that the very thing that bound us flung us apart, that my siblings often resented my attempts to bring us all together.

And sometimes children who grew up with a severely mentally ill parent may respond as my siblings did, avoiding all reminders of that painful time. That is another way to assert control. They probably did not realize that I was well-intentioned, that their rejection of me felt personal to me and was painful.

Growing up as I did, with mental illness the demanding, dominant member of my household, has shaped me and how I view life.

I believe that my childhood has also given me a gift of unusual perception and insight into human behavior.

Because
I have lived it
I have learned
To understand it.

CHAPTER NINE

My mother and her mental illness were the Siamese twins that lived in my childhood home. It is difficult to describe these two characters separately from one another, because her mental illness was usually firmly attached to her. I was able to see infrequent, brief glimpses of my mother without her mental illness, but it is fair to say that I really do not know much about my mother.

This is my description of my mother and her mental illness:

They can be very charming (but not for long).

It is violent and abusive.

She is petite and pretty.

It is big and scary.

It is paranoid.

She does not like to swear.

It often swears.

She likes to listen to baseball games while drinking wine and loves the Chicago Cubs.

She likes to read romance novels.

It thinks people are trying to kill her.

She likes cats and dogs, but not horses.

It has loud conversations with unseen people.

She used to say she had a headache to get out of social situations that made her uncomfortable.

It had a lot of headaches.

She is intelligent.

It often made no sense.

Her birth mother had severe mental illness.

Her birth mother was never discussed—*ever.*

She is an adopted, only child with a terrible childhood.

Her childhood was never discussed—*ever.*

It does not like children, including her own.

Her children's responses to her confuse her.

She takes great care in her grooming and appearance.

Its behavior is wildly erratic.

She is a devout Catholic.

It had extramarital affairs while married to my dad.

They don't know how to be a mom.

But sometimes she tried.

I don't think she knew how to be a wife.

But I think sometimes she tried.

She longed to be independent and have a career of her own.

They never stayed long at any job.

They have very few friends and no close friends.

I think she was lonely.

I think she desperately wanted to be normal.

I don't think she had any idea what being normal meant.

My mother was very confusing to me. She did none of the things that I thought a mom should do, and lots of things I knew a mom most definitely should NOT do.

My mother behaved the way she did because she is mentally ill.

Mental illness can be a ferocious disease. It lived in my mother, unchecked for the most part, and resulted in ferocious behavior.

She is this.
They are that.

They controlled.
She was lost.

That is sad.

Ferocity in.
Ferocity out.

CHAPTER TEN

The Siamese twins living in my home did not show themselves to many people. My mother is an attractive woman, and when she goes out in public she is well groomed and dresses stylishly. She likes to spend money on clothing and her appearance. She is intelligent. *She looks normal.*

She does not lurch around, unkempt, dirty. She does not scream at strangers or stare vacantly when spoken to. My mother learned how to deal with her illness by not letting people get to know her, and by staying home when she was acutely unwell. When I was growing up, her excuse for avoiding people and social situations was that she had a headache. I grew up thinking that my mother had enough headaches to qualify for the Guinness Book of World Records. I also grew up thinking that my mom's headaches could hit anytime, anywhere, and most often did so when the rest of us we were knee deep in fun somewhere. The announcement that my mother had a headache meant a quick evacuation from wherever we were to home.

People would have thought she was a bit strange, but on a broad scale of normalcy, she would have registered as normal. She didn't come across as shy, but as strange, antisocial, withdrawn. I remember her seeming wistful at times in social situations, as though she knew she could not fully participate but yearning to do so.

She had lapses. She would work somewhere for a while, quitting when people started to get to know her. She simply could not withstand the scrutiny. There were times that she would go out in public and have loud conversations with the voices that lived inside her head. She was less able to maintain the façade at extended family social events, like holidays and weddings, and when she started to crack, we all had to leave because of her inevitable headache.

My mother's appearance of normalcy was a two-edged sword. On the one hand, it helped us maintain the veneer of a "normal" family. We were able to avoid the stigma of having a mental illness living in our house. We were all accomplices in maintaining our secret, and my mother did her part to hide the existence of her severe mental illness from the outside world.

But the flip side of this appearance of normalcy was that none of us could get any help for the unrelenting collateral damage.

I recently found a picture of us taken for our church directory, all seven of us, scrubbed and polished, each of us playing our part in our collective lie—that we were a normal family. I study that picture and I wonder what was going through each of our heads at that time. In particular, I look at the forced, wan smile of my mother, and I wonder: was she overwhelmed? Did she realize the extent of her illness? Did she desperately want help? Surely her life must have been extremely difficult. Surely she was lonely, isolated as she was inside her head.

As I study each of our faces in that photograph I am able to see, now with the benefit of hindsight, that we were drawn together by one fundamental imperative: we were all trying our very best to survive.

Mirror mirror
we pretended so well.
People would not have known
we were living in hell.

CHAPTER ELEVEN

I am ten years old. At school I begin to feel unwell—nauseated, hot, sleepy, achy. I say nothing, hoping it will pass, hoping I don't commit the ultimate embarrassment of throwing up in class. I don't tell my teacher or go to the school nurse, the aged Mrs. O'Brien, who dozes off in her dusty cupboard behind the gymnasium, surrounded by Band-Aids and baby aspirin and glass jars with cotton balls and Q-tips. I know my mother will be angry if she has to come and get me from school, so I watch the clock and wait for the final bell.

On the school bus ride home I put my head down on my book bag, wishing I could lie down under a warm blanket and sleep.

When we get off the school bus my mother is in her bedroom, door locked. We know that means she does not want to be disturbed. My siblings crowd around the kitchen table to have cereal, squabbling while they eat our usual after-school snack. I feel too sick to join them and instead start to wash the pile of dirty dishes stacked up on the kitchen counter. My brother finishes first and goes downstairs to his room and then outside to do his farm chores.

I am envious of my brother, jealous that he has permission to leave the inside of the house when he is home. I know he has lots of responsibilities and the work on the farm is hard, but he has the freedom to work alone, with animals, in the fresh air. I watch him through the kitchen window as he trudges unenthusiastically to the silo, his head down in the biting winter cold, slipping and sliding on the ice and snow.

My baby sister, two years old, is in her playpen in the living room and welcomes the attention of her big sisters. It is my job to change her diaper, feed her, read to her, bathe her, take care of her. We all like to play with her. There is a pile of dirty dishes in the sink, and a note in my mother's handwriting instructs me to do my chores: wash the dishes, finish the laundry, clean up the kitchen and prepare supper. It is not written on the note, but I know my chores also include helping my sisters with their homework and making sure they have what they need for school tomorrow.

My mother doesn't write this because she doesn't have to, but in my mind I finish the note: "or I will be mad."

I am so sick that I start to cry, overwhelmed at the thought of the physical effort required to comply with my mother's instructions, wanting nothing more than to lie down and get warm. My nine-year-old sister Joan tells me she will help me, that it is best not to disturb mom, best if I get the chores done so mom doesn't get mad. Rose, at five and my mother's clear favorite, disappears into the basement playroom, her special dispensation from any household duties serving as an increasingly large wedge between us as we grow up.

By suppertime I am shivering, my head aches and my nausea has not abated. My father is working late, and sitting at the kitchen table with my brother and sisters, the overhead light blazing down on me, makes me feel worse. My mother emerges from her room to eat supper, and Joan tells her that I am sick. My mother acts as though she didn't hear, and Joan repeats herself. There is no response, and Joan looks at me quizzically and shrugs her shoulders. I ask my mother for permission to leave the table to go lie down. My mother's only response is to angrily ask why there is no bread on the table.

The phone rings, and my mother—her voice now strange and flirty—makes plans to meet someone in an hour. We are used to these calls. Uncharacteristically cheerful now, my mother gives me permission to go to my room and lie down. She scurries into her room, her dinner untouched, her children forgotten, and sometime later I hear her leave the house without saying a word to any of us.

I am cold and shivering and cannot get warm. I finally drag myself to the bathroom, blanket wrapped around me, and make a warm nest in the space under the sink where the bathroom heat register blows. My brother, worried, periodically comes in and anxiously asks me if I am okay.

I swim up from my feverish half-consciousness to my father standing above me at the sink cleaning his hands, my brother, frantic now, telling him that I am sick and have been sick all night. My father asks where I am, and I see shock turn to fear on his face as he bends down and sees me under the sink. He lifts me out and carries me to the car, all the time asking my brother where my mother is. I can smell diesel fuel and hay and silage and cow manure on his clothes—the smells of his work, the smells of our farm—and those smells make me feel strangely better. I sense my brother's anxiety as he trails behind my father to the garage, unable to answer where our mother is. I keep my eyes closed tight to the light, feel the worry coming off of my father in waves.

My father drives me straight to the hospital, checks me in, and then leaves, assuring me that he will be back. I spend that night and the next two in the hospital, the first time in my life I have spent the night separated from my family.

I am in pain. I am afraid. I want my mom and my dad. But not once do they come to see me. There is no phone in the stark room I am in, where I lie and look up at bare pipes in the ceiling, but I hear the phone ring periodically at the nurses' station outside my door. Each time it rings I strain to listen, hoping in vain that it is my parents with a message for me. I beg the nurses to call them. I explain to them through my tears that perhaps my parents don't know where I am, don't know how much I need them. It is a better rationale than the alternative, which is that they cannot be bothered driving thirty minutes to see their ten-year-old daughter in the hospital. The nurses and the doctor try to reassure me, but eventually become impatient with my crying and tell me to stop it.

But I cannot stop it. I cannot stop this feeling of being utterly abandoned. I don't think I will ever see my family again and that thought, confirmed by hour after hour of no visit, no phone call, becomes the only thing I can think about. I am completely distraught. As the hours and days pass I continue to weep, silently now, aware of the frowns exchanged between the nurses, their impatience with me, their whispered conversations outside my room.

My mother, strangely silent, finally shows up to take me home. I am overwhelmed with relief. The thirty-minute drive home is silent until the last five minutes, when she chastises me for getting sick and causing the family more trouble and expense. By the time we pull into the driveway she is working herself into a frenzy of anger at my diabolical need for attention and constant lack of consideration.

I get out of the car and flee to my room.

Fears irrational
Are devoid of fact.

Fears rational
Are based upon fact.

I was abandoned.
Fact.

My fear of abandonment
is therefore rational.

CHAPTER TWELVE

Brave soldiers, mortally wounded in battle, can be heard crying out for their mother. Grown men, courageous and strong, the person they call out for to comfort them and to be with them when they know they cannot survive in their broken, shredded bodies is often their mother. I wonder about that, wonder what in their being so wants and needs their mom. Can mom take away the horror of what happened? Ease the fear of dying? Provide relief from the pain of their wounds? Is there a strong, innate need for the person who cared for us from the beginning of our existence to be there at the end? What is it about our mother that causes us to instinctively want her in our hour of greatest need?

We all go through life as soldiers, facing our particular battles. And when the battle is most intense, that is when you want your mom.

That is precisely when you *need* your mom.

CATE GRACE

What I remember most about my hospitalization at the age of ten is that I cried and cried. My overwhelming sense of abandonment outweighed any physical discomfort. I've never forgotten it.

As a parent I have had to take my children to the hospital, where I stayed by their side, holding their hand, sleeping in a chair by the side of their bed. I would not dream of leaving them.

I found out later that my family told no one that I was in the hospital. My aunt was tearful when I told her about having had no visitors, how the nurses had scolded me and told me to stop crying. My hospitalization apparently rose to the level of yet another of many household secrets to be maintained, for a reason I cannot begin, even now, to comprehend. Not only did my parents abandon me to the hospital, but they ensured that no other friendly face came to visit me, either.

When I questioned my father about it years later, he vividly recalled how sick I was, his relief when the doctors told him I would be okay but needed to be hospitalized, and his worry and anger about where his wife was. When I asked him why they never came to see me he could only shrug helplessly and tell me he didn't have an answer.

My fear of abandonment continues to be part of who I am. As an adult it manifests in a number of ways, but always it is about my fear that I am irrelevant, that I will be left behind, that I have been forgotten, that I am not included—because I am not important and I do not matter. This wounding at times affects my relationships with my children, my siblings, my friends and colleagues, and usually comes across as a super sensitivity to how I am treated. The crux of the wounding is that I am not important and I do not matter. I am being thrown away, left behind.

Perhaps those soldiers on the battlefield know that their mother is the one person in their life who will never abandon them—and so they call for her in their hour of greatest need. On the few occasions in my adult life when I have called for my mother she has not responded. In the context of my mother, my sense of abandonment has transformed into a realization that I am not important to her and I do not matter to her. It is only with the benefit of time and maturity that I have been able to see that her mental illness dictates this response.

I have on two occasions invited my mother to share my joy in life-altering events. I sent her an invitation to my wedding. I knew she would not come, yet I searched for her in the crowd that day, part of me hoping to see her but intensely relieved that she was not there. It was such a strange, internally inconsistent feeling.

When my daughter was born I sent her a card, telling her that she had a grandchild, and inviting her to see the baby—this daughter of her own daughter—at her convenience, at any neutral location she wished. She never responded.

I again felt relief.

Why did I extend the olive branch and make the effort to invite her? I did so in the hope that something had changed. I held on to the hope that perhaps she would now love me. I hoped that we could finally have a real mother-daughter relationship. I did not really want her to come to my wedding or arrange to see my daughter. I wanted a mother to be with me when I married my husband, to celebrate my daughter and my motherhood with me. I hoped that the woman who birthed me and watched me grow up had somehow transformed into the mother I desperately wanted and needed, knowing full well that she had not. I knew that mental illness was still her constant companion, still whispering in her ear, sometimes shouting to get her full attention.

But I *hoped* anyway.

Growing up as I did, I constantly noticed the sanctity of the mother-daughter relationship. Like a person born without legs who cannot help but notice all those around her who are able to run and jump and walk, I was keenly aware from a very young age that something was wrong with my relationship with my mom. My most fervent desire was to have the sort of relationship with her that I observed mothers and daughters all around me had. And because I was a child, I assumed that the problem lay not with her, but with me.

It was an assumption I came to early in my life which was reinforced often and rarely negated.

I have had times in my life when I wanted **a** mother, but I have never wanted *my* mother. When I got married, and when my marriage ended, when I was ill, when I gave birth to my daughter, when I adopted my son, when I could not find my way, when I wanted and needed unconditional love and encouragement, that's when I really needed a mom.

I am no different than those brave soldiers on the battlefield.

But never have I wished for *my* mother.

If my own mother
can
leave me
forget about me
abandon me....
Anybody
can.

CHAPTER THIRTEEN

I am forty-four. I am having my weekly coffee with my friend Mark. Mark is ten years older than me, single, never married, no children. A university professor, Mark lives inside his head and intellectualizes his place in the world. He is the writer of political commentary and treatises on economics, politics and power.

Mark avoids most people, finding them all a bit too silly for the real problems of the world and the need for immediate and genuine solutions. I am pleased that Mark appreciates my company and that I am not one of the vast majority of humans Mark finds "too silly" to be his friend.

We are discussing one of our regular topics: Mark's less-than-perfect childhood. It is some of the glue of our relationship. Mark knows that I have no relationship with my mother at all, difficult relationships with my siblings, that my dad and I have had to work hard to rehabilitate our relationship and that I attribute this to my mother's raging mental illness. It has been a relief to have a friend like Mark with whom I can talk about my childhood.

While we may have both experienced difficult childhoods, we do not share a common reaction to our dysfunctional past. Mark still acts like the great victim of his childhood, blaming his adult misfortune on his parents, and he is launching into another tirade, this time blaming his parents for his lack of tenure at the university. I usually enjoy these discussions, as they help me to not feel so isolated in my own difficult childhood, and I realize that I am leaps and bounds ahead of Mark in my ability to put the effects of my childhood into context.

Mark has never shared the specifics of his childhood. I have always had the impression that he grew up with erratic, irrational parenting and abuse, based upon his descriptions to me of his childhood experiences and reinforced by aspects of him that are clearly damaged.

As I listen to him today, I cannot understand how he connects his lack of tenure to his childhood.

"What specifically was so bad about your childhood?" I ask him when he takes a breath.

"My parents abused me," he responds plaintively.

"What exactly did they do to you?" I ask.

I realize that I am potentially treading on dangerous ground.

"They never understood me. They abused me. They constantly criticized my long hair and my political views. They hated the music I listened to."

I press on.

"What else, Mark? I mean, you were in high school in the 1960s; everyone had long hair and radical political views and listened to music nobody's parents liked."

"I know they loved me. They told me they loved me. But they never understood me, Cate. They didn't even try to."

I am dumbfounded and can't help but feel as though Mark's parents are not the only ones who did not understand him.

"But did they ever physically assault you? Did they neglect you? Mentally abuse you? Verbally berate you?"

Horrified, he assures me that they had never done any of those things, and repeats that he always knew his parents loved him but that they abused him because they did not try to understand him.

I look at him across the table. I see him with my new eyes. He is a broken man because in the late 1960s his parents did not approve of his long hair and he felt they never really understood him.

I am speechless.

So what? My brain is screaming. *So what!*

CATE GRACE

Searching for your truth
by
gazing into the mirrors of others
while helpful
is not always accurate.

Search for your truth
within your own perfect heart.

Your truth is neither
right
nor
wrong.
It simply is.

CHAPTER FOURTEEN

Like most parents, I would, without thought or hesitation, sacrifice myself to save my children. My natural instinct would take over, an instinct stronger than my own need to survive. From that powerful experience of our collective instinct, we as a human race believe that the parent-child relationship is sacred and special.

What happens when the natural course has gone horribly awry, when the mother, rather than protecting her children, is the source of all kinds of dangers to their little bodies, minds, and spirits?

What powerful force could cause the disruption of that deep, basic instinct?

Mental illness is powerful enough to disrupt the natural order. Mental illness has no regard for the inviolability of human relationships or the natural order of things. Heartless, soulless, mental illness tears through the fabric of human relationships effortlessly, indiscriminately.

I have discovered that the reality of mental illness is very difficult for people to comprehend. Its ability to destroy relationships that society deems sacred and unbreakable is boundless. The collateral damage is deep and far-reaching.

Most people don't understand the depth and breadth of what happens to a child when a parent has severe mental illness. It's not their fault, because much of it is incomprehensible. I can tell you with utter certainty that it is much more than not approving of a hairstyle or disagreeing about politics. My mother's disease was omnipresent and affected all aspects of our lives. It was everything.

It was all I knew. *The collateral damage caused by mental illness was all I knew.* It affected all aspects of my relationship with both my parents. It affected my relationships with my siblings. It affected how I felt about myself, and how I interacted with my peers. It affected every aspect of my life. It continues to affect me now, more than thirty years after I last lived in that home.

Well-intentioned people have encouraged me to "make up" with my mother, as though we had an argument about politics or my choice of a husband. I have been told by others—also well intentioned—that I will have "regrets" when she dies. I now realize that these people, like Mark, equate growing up with a severely mentally ill mother with an argument about hair style and music and the battle cry of all teenagers that their parents don't understand them.

Worse yet is the mindset of these well-intentioned people that with the maturity and knowledge of my adult mind will come an extraordinary and sympathetic understanding of those childhood years. Armed with the magic wand of that comprehension, I will be able to embrace my mother as she really is and wave away those years as though they never happened. I can then start a fresh relationship with my mom, a relationship deeply rooted in empathy for her condition and an awareness of my reactions to it. We can have a normal and loving mother-daughter relationship.

This mindset ignores the essence of the parent-child relationship, disregards the inherent inequity of the relationship, the enormous influence wielded by even a very ill parent over her child. It is the very nature of this unique relationship that not only binds, but destroys.

I understand that I should feel sympathy for my mother. My brain tells me that she suffers from an illness, so that what happened was not her fault. While my brain can tell me what to think, I can only look to my heart to examine how I feel.

I realize that a daughter should feel many things for her mother. I have never experienced those feelings. I have experienced other, equally profound emotions springing from my relationship with my mother. And so I am content with this: mental illness can turn the parent-child relationship upside down and inside out. The result cannot be defined by what I *should* feel, but what I *do* feel.

Getting to this point has been a struggle. Human beings have deep-seated, firmly-held beliefs, beliefs that bind us together and define us as members of the same human family no matter our color, our religion, our socio-economic status, or our culture. Many of those profound beliefs center around our relationships with one another: taking something that is not yours is stealing, killing another person is generally wrong, parents love their children, children love and respect their parents. These beliefs are deeply, culturally rooted and reinforced constantly through social media, the news, marketing, movies, television, novels, art. Observe, for example, during the course of just one week how many times we are reminded that a mother's love for her child is unconditional—or should be.

Not only do I have to step past those ancient, instinctive, sacred beliefs that I myself hold, but I have to face the fact that other people, no matter how well intentioned, cannot understand how irrevocably broken my relationship with my mother is. I have to learn to trust and believe in myself and what I know to be my personal truth. In doing so, I must rely upon my feelings to guide me, acknowledging that they are not right or wrong, they simply *are*.

I have come to understand that most people simply cannot grasp the effect mental illness has had on my relationship with my mother. Well-intentioned people cannot know or understand the incomprehensible.

I do know this: I won't have regrets when she dies.

I've already had them.

You say
this is what it should be.

I say
this is what it is.

And the two
are not
even
close.

CHAPTER FIFTEEN

I am twelve years old. My brother, sister and I run off the school bus, racing each other to the house, play hitting each other as we run, shouting, boisterous from our day at school and from the warm, spring sun. Just for these moments, as we race each other, laughing, I feel happy and carefree and deeply connected to them.

We know as soon as the door opens and the smells of freshly baked cookies waft out: Aunt Veronica is here! My two youngest sisters are already sitting at the table, legs swinging in the big chairs; my four-year-old baby sister is sitting on the phone book to reach the table; still-warm cookies and cold glasses of red Kool Aid are waiting for us.

"We waited for you so we could all have our snack together," my youngest sister says, clearly proud of her self-control.

Veronica, always smiling, always fun, gives each of us a deep satisfying hug and sends us down the hall to wash our hands before we sit down together.

We do not question her presence or ask where our mother is. When we left the house for school that day the house was filthy, my father grim, my mother still in her dark bedroom where she had been the last many days. I look around as I race my siblings to the bathroom to wash our hands. The house smells like Lysol, everything is clean, the windows are open and the fresh spring air blows gently through the curtains, causing them to rise and gently fall. I peek into my bedroom and see that the beds are freshly made and the room is neat and tidy. The bathroom glistens, and through the window I see freshly washed laundry hanging on the line outside.

Veronica asks us each how our day at school was, and even my brother, now a quiet teenage boy, responds with uncharacteristic enthusiasm with a story about the high school principal's temper tantrum that day. I am so happy that I feel my body buzzing, and I cannot stop smiling. We chatter and laugh and tease one another, and I find myself back in my familiar fantasy of hoping that this will never end, that Veronica will stay with us forever.

Veronica finally asks us about our homework and sits at the table with us as we pull it out of our bookbags. She helps us with it, except for the math, which she says is like Greek to her. When we finish it and put it back into our bookbags, she tells us to go and play so she can get supper going.

Not one of us asks where my mother is or when she will be coming back.

The next minute feels like ten as we collectively watch my youngest sister carefully get off her chair and drape herself on Veronica's lap, asking Veronica to please read a story to her. We all freeze, waiting for her reaction. We three oldest are too old for stories to be read to us, but I desperately want to sit next to Veronica while she reads a story—any story—to us. I know I am a big baby for wanting something so stupid, but my brother and two other sisters have the same hopeful look on their faces.

Veronica's eyes fill with tears, and she reaches into her blouse for the inevitable stash of tissues she keeps there. "Wouldn't you rather go outside and play in the sun?" she asks, as she turns away from us to wipe her eyes and blow her nose. She keeps her head turned away for what seems a long time, and we are uncomfortable and silent. We have upset Veronica, but I am not sure why, or what to do about it.

My sister Joan breaks the awkward silence by loudly announcing that she is going outside to practice pulling wheelies on her bicycle. Veronica turns back to us, her eyes red and bright now, and promises us that she will read to us after supper if we like.

I offer to help with supper and ask Veronica what my chores are, but Veronica tells me I have the night off and to go have fun. I notice her eyes are red and tearful again, and I wonder what I have done to upset her with my offer of help. I tell her that I am sorry, and her tears spill out now as she reassures me that I have done nothing wrong, that she is thinking about something sad that is making her cry. She shoos me out of the kitchen and I run out to play in the late afternoon sun.

Suppertime is wonderful. My father is relaxed and funny, and Veronica, my dad's older sister, tells us hilarious stories about him as a little boy. They tease each other and we all laugh. We sit at the table long after we are done eating and I notice my body buzzing again. I am so happy.

Veronica reads to my baby sister after we do the dishes and clean up. My brother and I pretend we are not listening, but we are. Sue sits on Veronica's lap, and Rose and Joan sit as close to Veronica as they can. I wish I wasn't twelve years old. I wish I could sit on Veronica's lap and have her read to me, but I am too old for such things.

My father sits at the kitchen table reading the mail and paying bills. I go out and sit next to him and tell him about my day, about how I want to be a veterinarian when I grow up, or maybe a horse jockey, but definitely not a nurse or a teacher, about how my friend at school is moving away, about how Sister Bernadine, the piano teacher, fell asleep and snored during my piano lesson again. I love talking to my wise and funny father. He pushes away the mail and the bills and we talk and laugh. This is a treat we are not allowed when my mother is home, and I bask in the undivided attention of my father and the feeling that I am special and wonderful.

Not once do any of us ask where our mother is.

After Veronica tucks us into bed I am aware of the peace in the house, of how comfortable I am, and once again the buzzing envelopes my body. I pray over and over again for Veronica to never leave, for my mother to never come back.

As I start to drift off I hear my father and Veronica talking softly in the kitchen, hear my father say, "What else can I do?" and Veronica's soft voice in reply.

I do not know if Veronica will be waiting for us tomorrow after school, but I know that she will be there when I wake up in the morning. I relax and fall asleep.

Glimpses of
how it could be
how it should be
helped me
to hold on.

CHAPTER SIXTEEN

Before I was born, my mother was admitted to the state mental hospital. While there, she underwent the first of several courses of electro-convulsive (shock) therapy. She was medicated, and since she was under constant medical supervision to take her medication, her condition improved. She was then discharged home, apparently "cured."

This pattern repeated while I was growing up. My mother would go away. My aunt would come to stay with us, and life was achingly normal for a too-short period of time. Veronica was an excellent mother to us, and I often fantasized that she would just stay on and become our "real" mother. When Veronica was there, laundry was done, the house was clean, regular wholesome meals were on the table. Best of all, I was tucked into bed at night with love. I felt safe and loved and cared for.

Then my mother would come home, and Veronica would go back to her wonderfully normal home. Initially my mother was a zombie. We were very careful around her, as we did not want to disturb her. She was completely absent from us. She was the shell of a human being. She slept a lot. She talked not at all. She sat and did nothing, staring straight ahead, unable to contribute to the endless chores it took to maintain that household full of people.

And then one day that would end, and we would come into the house to find her screaming and flushing medication down the toilet. Sure that she was being poisoned, she would destroy all medication, blaming us, our father, and anyone else she could think of. There was no reasoning with her.

My parents were devout Catholics like the vast majority of everyone in that Irish-German area. They lived on a farm outside a town with a population of about 50,000 people.

The local Catholic priest, hearing about one of my mother's early hospitalizations for mental health treatment, drove out to the farm to see my father to discuss the hospitalization with him. He reminded him that marriage meant that a spouse did not do what my father had done, that my father was to stand by my mother, through sickness and in health, not dump her conveniently off at the hospital when things got a little rough. My father said very little.

Some weeks after my mother came home from the hospital, the effects of the shock treatment and medication wore off. She flew into a rage, locking my father out of the house, and using a baseball bat, broke windows, doors, walls, and furniture. My father, helpless, tried to plead with her from outside a broken window.

Finally, he drove the few miles to church, persuaded the priest to come with him, and silently drove back to the house, the bewildered priest next to him. The two men sat in the pickup truck while my mother railed inside the house, cursing, screaming, demolishing the inside of the house and its contents.

There was silence in the truck for several minutes. Eventually, my father turned to the priest and asked him what he thought he should do. The priest, horrified, could only respond, "Pray, my son, you must pray."

The priest's suggestion to my father to pray was as good a response as any at that time. In Middle America in the 1960s, decent society did not openly discuss mental illness. Decent people did not behave like my mother. People watched the Andy Griffin show, laughed at Carol Burnett's antics, listened to Walter Cronkite every night. I grew up in the Midwest of America, where people still live in rural agricultural communities. People are conservative, private, sensible. Social situations were—and still are— peppered with detailed discussions ascertaining the genealogical lineage of everyone in attendance, as well as anyone else whose name comes up in the conversation. This is both fascinating and hilarious.

"You know Jack Kleinschoft, don't you?
Yes, yes, I know you do.
His father and Ray Goughan are cousins.
That's right, Ray's mother and Jack's father are brother and sister.
They lived over on the old Hanson place for years.
Next to Mrs. Sherman.
She owned the whole place, rented it out after the Hansons died.
She was Mr. Hanson's sister, you see, never married again after Cliff never came back from the war.

Cliff was her husband. That's right, Cliff was awarded the Purple Heart.
Shame what's happening over in Viet Nam...
Dayton Marshall's son's over there now.
No, the second oldest one.
The oldest one is married to Jack Kleinschoft's second or third daughter.
I can't think of her first name...
Yeah, that's right, Danita."

These conversations would go on and on, and were endlessly interesting for the adults and endlessly boring for children.

We children would tune out unless the voices of the adults dropped conspiratorially, at which point we knew something juicy was coming. Usually that meant a conversation about a child born out of wedlock, infidelity within our community, alcoholism, an impending death due to cancer.

Or mental illness.

If adults could not talk about it except in whispers, what hope did we children have of coping with it?

Secrets secrets
Whispered low
Shame attaches
Where whispers go.

CHAPTER SEVENTEEN

What my mother's mental illness meant to me was that her mood could change in the time it took her to walk from the living room to the kitchen. She was entirely unpredictable. She was often disconnected from reality, communicating loudly and aggressively, or in loud whispers and knowing nods, with beings none of the rest of us could see.

She did not sleep, wandering the house in the dark, night after night. She was incapable of caring for the children she had, yet continued to bring babies home. She could be violent and abusive. She never hugged me, held me, told me she loved me. She never cared for me, nor about me, and she told me so. She dreamt up elaborate plans revolving around a desire on the part of others, sometimes us, to kill her. She assumed any conversation not including her was about her.

As teenagers, we hated going out in public with her. If we went to the one shopping mall in town, we kids trailed behind her as far as we dared. The trick in the shopping mall was to fall back far enough that people weren't sure we were with her, but close enough that she assumed we were simply falling behind.

Not that she always noticed. Sometimes she was so deeply engrossed in a conversation with invisible people, conducted in loud, sometimes violent, stage whispers that she did not notice how we fell farther and farther behind, horrified that someone we knew would see us. If she discovered us and believed that we were deliberately lagging, she accused us of making her walk in front of us so she could be the target for some unseen assassin.

What mental illness in my house meant to me was that my mother could not form normal emotional bonds with her children. With the onset of each pregnancy—and there were many more pregnancies than babies in that house—her symptoms worsened. She had many first-trimester miscarriages, and it was in the immediate aftermath of a miscarriage that my mother was the nicest to us. I was alone with her in the house when she miscarried once. I witnessed her crying, real tears and real emotion, and she actually talked to me about the heartache of losing this child, a tiny being she had already named Stephanie.

That was the only time I ever got a glimpse into her heart.

It was the only time she ever spoke to me like that.

It was lovely.

With the birth of each child her symptoms worsened. (The effect of this on my father cannot be underestimated. A few years after my daughter was born, my father confessed that he had lived in fear that I would develop mental illness as a result of my pregnancy). I realize now how absolutely logical it was for her to ultimately blame the child for her agony. Effect did follow cause. Pregnancy and the resulting child caused the symptoms of her mental illness to spike, sometimes out of control. There was an order to what was happening. Given that logic, her treatment of us was, at some level, reasonable.

When the fourth child came along, my mother took that infant girl, Rose, and walked down the gravel road into nowhere. My father searched and searched for her, but could not find her. Some days later she walked back, wearing the same clothes, silent, carrying a strangely silent baby, offering no explanation as to where she'd been. When Rose developed the familiar symptoms as a young adolescent, I wondered if my mother had taken her to some secret initiation ceremony during that time they disappeared down that road.

Now I understand
at least a little bit:
I came along
You felt like crap
Therefore
I made you feel
like crap.

CHAPTER EIGHTEEN

I am ten years old. It is the first day of school. I am beginning fifth grade.

But this is no ordinary first day of school. Last night we moved into our new house thirty miles away from my childhood home and everything I have ever known. We will be attending a large public school. We will be riding a school bus rather than in a car pool with neighbors. I know no one at this new school, and I am terrified. Until now I have always attended the small Catholic school ten miles from my house.

I am, by nature, shy. There has never been a need for me to be anything other than shy. I have attended school with the same twenty-one children for the past five years. We all know one another. Our parents know one another. Our grandparents know one another. I have had a set of ready-made friends from the moment I was born, by virtue of our breeding and the sheer repetition of seeing each other year after year.

I am worried. I know I do not have the social skills to make new friends and I will be an outsider and a loner. I see myself clearly in this new school as the social outcast, the new girl who is smart (not a positive characteristic) and unattractive and unlikable.

At the age of ten, there is no worse fate.

My brother and sisters and I wait for the school bus outside our home. We are all quiet and nervous. We are all tired from our big house move the day before. We have never ridden a school bus before.

We are all scared. My stomach hurts.

When the bus pulls up, I want to run away and hide in the barn. Instead, we all troop onto the half-empty bus, mumbling our hellos to the cheerful bus driver.

As the bus continues its route my anxiety increases. By the time the bus stops at the long concrete driveway in front of the school I am frantically searching my brain for a strategy to overcome the fate I am certain is mine.

And then it dawns on me. I can survive at this new school if I can make new friends. I can make new friends if I am outgoing. The problem is that I am shy, which means that I will not be able to make new friends.

But nobody at this school knows me. Nobody at this school knows that I am shy. I will, therefore, pretend that I am not shy. I will pretend that I am outgoing. And I will be able to make new friends and survive at this new school.

I will survive this.

I step off the bus, walk the long concrete driveway to the building, and become Cate the Outgoing.

When presented
with
an enormous bowl of lemons
Sometimes
You can make lemonade.

CHAPTER NINETEEN

Growing up with a mentally ill parent does not define me. I am the writer of short stories and poems and a half-finished novel. I am the single mother of two children. I teach yoga. I am a lawyer and an advocate. I am an immigrant. I am a sister, a friend, a daughter, a niece. I am a healer. I live in a beautiful old house that needs constant attention. I love my dog and my cats.

What I am not is this: I am not a "victim" of anything. Most people who know me would never dream that my past is anything but ordinary.

I used to think it was obvious that something was different about me. I could see the shattered parts of myself when I looked in the mirror, and I assumed that others could, too. Throughout my teens and well into my twenties, I was always surprised that even after getting to know me, my friends still liked me. However, I have very few friends from those years. It was always me who drifted away from those friends, certain that if they got to know me they would discover that I was not worthy of their friendship and reject me.

It was much easier for me to simply fade out of their life before they discovered the real me.

It wasn't that I didn't always have lots of friends—just that I had trouble keeping them. I figured out how to make friends. I know, in fact, precisely when I learned how to do that.

It was when I began the fifth grade.

Until our move we lived in a rural area where my father's relatives lived. People with my last name lived there for at least four generations, and they were good people, known in that rural farming area for their generous nature and bad fences. Livestock wandering on the roads and on other people's land was the result of a genetic inability on the part of my relatives to construct a proper fence. Even as a child I could see what the problem was: people with my surname used bits of wire and odd pieces of junk to cobble something together that presented no challenge to any livestock with a desire to see a bit of the world or test the theory about the greenness of the grass on the other side of the fence. I used to look admiringly at the fences of our friends and neighbors—tall, straight, solid, with matching pieces that did not fall over in a strong wind.

A person's surname was their social and business introduction: McNamaras were fun, happy people who loved to drink. Kleinstopfs were misers. Nolans were hard workers and Findlers couldn't be trusted. Graces were good folks, but hopeless at building fences.

An amazing thing happened on my first day at that big, new school, something that I believe only happened because severe mental illness resided in my house. I would survive at this new school if I could make new friends, which I could do if I pretended to be outgoing.

I was good at pretending; I pretended there was nothing wrong with my mother; I pretended my family was normal.

I was good at surviving.

It worked. I grew into the person I pretended to be that day. People use many adjectives to describe me, but "shy" is not one of them.

I was able to rise above myself to survive because severe mental illness lived in my house. Living with mental illness taught me to think in a very sophisticated manner about my options. Living with mental illness taught me to pretend to be someone I was not.

But what one hand gave, the other took away. Though I became very socially skilled, I knew that if my friends really knew me, they would not like me.

If my own mother could not love me, who could?

I am many things
because of this
and
in spite of this
but
I am not broken.

CHAPTER TWENTY

Moving to our new house caused my mother to become more unstable. Any change was difficult for her. We moved from a large four-bedroom home to a crowded, smaller, three-bedroom house. We moved away from friends and my father's extended family to a completely new area, surrounded by strangers. My father told me years later that he thought moving away would help my mother, because she did not seem to fit in with the people he grew up with. A fresh start with new people they would get to know together seemed like a good idea at the time. Of course my father did not know, could not anticipate, how our housemate—mental illness, would respond.

It wasn't that my mother moved away from her family and friends. An only child, she had no brothers, sisters, nieces, nephews. She had very little contact with her adoptive parents. I don't remember her ever telephoning her mother and father just to talk. In fact, I don't recall her ever telephoning anyone just for a chat.

Maybe what happened when we moved was that the unwanted member of our family—mental illness—took up more space in that new house. Perhaps in the closer quarters, with all of us children growing up and needing more space of our own, the presence of mental illness in our home became more obvious to us all. I know that mental illness is a selfish housemate under the best of circumstances.

It was here, in our new home, that I began to understand some of the bizarre circumstances of our household. The move coincided with my own pre-adolescence, that magical time when you are able to see clearly into the adult world with the wide-open eyes of a child. Prior to our move I knew only that something was terribly wrong in our house, but I could not express what it was. After we moved and my mother's behavior became more pronounced, I could at least start to name some of the things that made us completely unlike other families.

We lived on a farm in a rural area, our neighbors a quarter of a mile away. We were all farmers, by nature optimistic and friendly. My father had no trouble meeting people and making friends. It was in this new social environment that I first become aware of the social disability wrought by my mother's mental illness and the collateral damage of that disability to us all.

My father was a personable, fun-loving man. He was the parent who made me laugh, comforted me when I was sick or scared, and took the time to talk to me. When I related a problem to him or asked him for his help or advice, he would often rub his chin, get a twinkle in his eye, and preface his discussion with a very serious, "Back when I was a little girl...." When I was very young, I believed that my father was an authority on all things feminine because he had once been a little girl himself.

When we moved to our new home my father had to change the essence of who he was in order to keep his marriage and his family together. We moved from a community that had known my father all his life and was accepting of his bizarre and unpredictable wife. There was something unspoken about their support of us, due to our paternal bloodline. Perhaps it was that they knew my father in his own right, and based upon that, they were willing to overlook my mother's strange behavior.

My father went from an outgoing sociable man, who loved to have fun, to a man who worked all the time and was often tired. When my parents occasionally went out to community events, they often came home early due to my mother's headaches.

My father's responses to my mother's behaviors were driven by a desire to attain—and maintain—peace in a violent and unpredictable household. He acquiesced to my mother's bizarre rants, demands and arguments, he became less social, he focused on work, he avoided being home. Looking back now I can see that this fun-loving, family-focused man became an absentee father as a result of my mother's mental illness. He played his part in pretending that all was well in our home. I have come to realize how painful it must have been for him.

It was hard to pretend it all away. Family social events resulting in any of us having fun were frowned upon by my mother. She threw dark disapproving stares at us if we laughed loudly, danced with abandon, openly enjoyed ourselves. She told us it was embarrassing that we "carried on" like that. And she didn't save those comments for the privacy of the ride home in the car. Sometimes she announced them to anyone who was listening. Other times she withdrew, refusing to speak to anyone in her vicinity, responding only with a flat monosyllable, if at all, to people who tried to speak to her.

I remember going to a cousin's wedding when I was eleven years old. The reception was held in a church hall, with a wedding dinner of ham and turkey from a buffet line for the guests. After the meal a band played, and the front of the hall was converted to a dance floor. The adults were drinking beer, we children were downing Coca Cola and root beer in enormous quantities, and I was surrounded by family and friends. I had a really great time.

Yet what I remember most clearly now, all these years later, is looking at my mother, sitting by herself at a long table, alone, angry, sullen, withdrawn. In the midst of that joyful celebration, there sat my mother, an island of isolated unhappiness.

My mother is
not this
and
not that.

My mother is
so different
as to be
completely alone
in her difference.

And that must be
very lonely.

CHAPTER TWENTY-ONE

I have just turned six years old. My birthday gift is a beautiful pink bike with a banana seat and a rainbow of colored streamers attached to the ends of the handlebars. A little license plate on the back has my name on it. The wheels have colored spokes, so when the wheels turn there is a blur of pink, blue, green, yellow and purple.

The bike is pure magic, the most lovely thing I have ever had. My dad gave it to me, his smile reaching his eyes when he saw my reaction. He told me that when he was a little girl he always wanted a bike just like this, so he thought I might like it. I marvel at how much like me my dad was when he was a little girl, and how lucky I am that he is my dad. I am so happy. I cannot wait to ride it.

It is a beautiful spring day. The warm sun shines down on Joan and me. We are riding my wonderful new bike up and down the road in front of our house. Joan is on the back of the banana seat, and I am in the front. We are laughing as we go back and forth, swerving around, doing quick turns, going fast, braking hard. The streamers swirl past my hands and sparkle in the sun. Joan hangs on tight to me as we put the bicycle through its paces. We laugh and laugh.

We live in the country, our nearest neighbor a mile away, and rarely is there traffic on our gravel road. We aim for the middle of the road, where there is less gravel, and ride, ride, ride in the warm sun, with the wheels a kaleidoscope of color, the handlebar streamers a shimmering rainbow. To get the full impact of the beauty of this bicycle, from time to time one of us gets off to admire the other one ride.

My mother comes to the door of the house and calls us in for a treat of freshly baked cookies. It is the only thing that can take us away from our fun.

We carefully set the bicycle on its kickstand at the top of the driveway and run into the house. When we get into the house, she pulls us in brusquely and closes the door, locking it. The bright sunshine of the spring day is shut out, with all the curtains pulled tightly.

Without a word, she marches us back into the back bedroom. She demands that we strip from the waist down. Joan and I are both scared and crying and asking what we have done wrong. My mother's face is once again a big black hole for a mouth and two small black holes for eyes. Our crying seems to make her more angry. She does not respond to our questions about what we have done wrong. She pulls out one of my father's big leather belts and starts to snap it in the air. I am so scared that I have to concentrate not to wet myself. Joan and I look at each other, and I see the pure terror consuming me mirrored in her eyes.

Then my mother beats us with one of our father's leather belts. "Strapping" is what she calls it as she screams out words that make no sense. I cannot understand why my mother is so angry, why she is punishing us, why she does not stop. My mother screams and straps us so long that we both eventually stop crying. I feel as though I am floating above myself watching this happen. I am numb.

When my dad comes in from his farm work that night for dinner, Joan and I are very quiet. Sitting is painful, and we shift uncomfortably throughout the meal. As the silent, uncomfortable meal wears on, I notice that Joan has tears streaming down her face, but she makes no sound. Her face is eerily expressionless.

My father asks what is wrong, what has happened, why Joan is crying. We are silent. He asks again, louder, and I look quickly at my mother, who glares at me. I look down and say nothing. The rest of the meal is enveloped in a thick, heavy, strained silence.

When my father tucks us into bed that night he asks Joan and me again, softly this time, "What is wrong?" He assures us that nothing bad will happen to us if we tell him and he wants to make sure that we are okay. I finally tell him, and both Joan and I choke back deep shuddering sobs as we relive the afternoon. My father examines our bruised, lacerated backsides and legs and his face grows dark and furrowed. He asks us over and over again what we did to make her angry. We have no answer for him. He kisses us goodnight and tells us he will take care of it, to not worry.

Joan and I are not able to sleep because of the violent argument we hear in the kitchen. My mother is screaming, my father is yelling. Doors slam. Silence ensues, and then the argument starts anew. This goes on for several hours.

I am worried the next day. My father is already gone by the time we wake up. My mother does not emerge from her bedroom. We go to school, and when we get home I walk up the driveway with dread in my stomach. I have a bad feeling about things. Joan and I hold hands as we go in the house. My mother is in her bedroom, the door shut. She opens the door and calls Joan and me to her room. Her voice is strangely monotone and flat. We pretend not to hear her and look at each other, desperate for a plan, and quickly start to go outside. We are still holding hands.

My mother runs to the kitchen and drags us back to her bedroom and shuts the door. The curtains are drawn and the room is dark and the big belt is the only thing on the bed. It is there like a snake, coiled for attack. I know from this day forward this belt will always make me feel like wetting myself, that this piece of thick leather and buckle will be one of the favorite weapons of choice of my mother. Somehow I know that this belt and I have only just begun our relationship of hatred. My mother sees the power of this belt over us, and she will capitalize upon it for years to come.

In the same strange, controlled monotone voice she demands to know which of us told our father about our punishment the day before. Neither of us answers her. I can feel the terror coming off Joan in waves, and I feel terror spilling out of me, filling the room. She tells us in that strange voice, fine, she will strap both of us. I cannot watch Joan being strapped again, and so I tell her that I am the one who told Dad. I cannot look at Joan.

She straps me over and over again with the belt and makes Joan watch. I beg and beg her not to, and when I realize that my begging means nothing, I grit my teeth hard and tell myself not to make a sound, not to cry. I concentrate on pretending that it does not hurt, telling myself that she enjoys it more when I cry, so I will be silent. Once again I float above myself and watch, which makes it easier to stay quiet as she beats and beats me.

My mother's voice is controlled and level as she repeats over and over again that she is strapping me because I told my dad. She warns me to never, ever, do so again. Not once does she raise her voice.

She is not the clawed monster with black holes for eyes and mouth.

She is someone else. Someone even more frightening.

She is the picture of controlled fury.

I never tell my dad again.

He never asks.

I had a recurring nightmare
for most of my childhood
A little man chases me
around a tree stump,
axe in hand
trying to cut off my head.

I run and run
fear and panic
fueling my legs
enveloping my body
screaming from my brain.

CHAPTER TWENTY-TWO

When I was a young teen, I watched the movie "Sybil." I was fascinated. An avid reader, I immediately obtained the book from the library. I could not stop myself from quickly reading page after page of the abuse the girl endured at the hands of her mother. I was fascinated by the multiple personalities that emerged from within this one, tiny woman, personalities all borne of the instinctive need to survive in spite of terrific odds.

What I connected with was the physical abuse at the hands of the one person Sybil was meant to be safe with. The sadism was way too familiar to me. The emotional abuse hit me in my guts. That no adult ever stopped it, ever saved Sybil from the raging of her mother, fit me like a second skin. And though the movie centered around Sybil's mental illness, the untold back story was the obvious untreated mental illness of Sybil's mother.

I remember a counselor once telling me with genuine sympathy that she understood what I'd been through, that it was just like growing up with an alcoholic parent. Eager to latch onto what I desperately needed, which was someone who understood, I quickly agreed.

But growing up with a mentally ill parent is nothing like growing up with an alcoholic parent. When your mother is an alcoholic, you quickly learn that when she drinks, her behavior changes. Effect follows cause.

When your mother is mentally ill, there is no rhyme or reason for behavioral changes. When your mother is an alcoholic, her behavior, though still somewhat unpredictable, likely has a pattern to it; the pattern begins with her drinking. When your mother is mentally ill, you have no idea how she will act, nor do you know what prompts the behavior.

So while I in no way mean to diminish the hardship of growing up with an alcoholic parent, at least with an alcoholic there is a degree of foreseeability. She drinks, she gets drunk, she acts a certain way. Effect follows cause.

With the mental illness in our house anything could happen. Anytime. Without warning. Without cause. My childhood home was chaotic and unpredictable. One ongoing effect of that is an underlying sense of anxiety based upon a belief that life is utterly unpredictable.

My father was overwhelmed with a seriously ill wife and three small children to care for, and two more to eventually arrive. There was never enough money. His response was to leave, justifying his hours away from our house by working and claiming that it could all be better if we only had more money.

My father has his own story of living with severe mental illness. He was married during a time and in a place where divorce was unheard of, and children lived with their mother, no matter what. Mental illness was stigmatizing. Treatment for mental illness was crude and hit and miss. I cannot tell his story for him. I can only tell the part that I know, the part that affected me: He ran away from it, leaving early in the morning, returning late at night, leaving us children behind under the guise of a need to work long hours in order to get ahead and make our lives better.

My father was never mean to me. I always knew he loved me. He tried to get help for my mother. There was absolutely no support for him in that endeavor.

He left me there, unprotected.

So I never had an adult to save me from my raging mother. Just like Sybil.

I can do nothing
(he realizes with despair)
there is nothing I can do.

If I am not here
(he whispers to himself)
I cannot know it.

If I do not know it
(he reasons to himself)
then it does not exist.

If it does not exist
(he convinces himself)
there is nothing for me to do.

And so I am not here.

CHAPTER TWENTY-THREE

With the mental illness that resided in my home, as long as my mother was conscious and in my vicinity, anything could happen. And so I was on constant alert. I become expert at quickly assessing any situation, reading body language, having various options for escaping any situation. This skill is a positive from my childhood, resulting in an ability for strategic thinking and group facilitation that is quite natural for me.

But my continuous hypervigilance in my own home did not stop when I went to bed at night. Nighttime was sometimes the most frightening time in our house.

My mother often did not sleep at night. She crept around at all hours, stealthy, catlike. Sometimes I would awaken, startled, and see her standing in the room my sister and I shared, a dark figure, silhouetted by the moonlight, staring at us as we slept. It was terrifying.

It is only now, having myself gazed in wonder at my own sleeping children in the quiet of the night, that I understand why I was so afraid of awakening to that empty, resentful stare in the darkness of the still, deep night. It is when I look at my children sleeping in the peacefulness of the night that I love them the most. No matter what they've done, or how bad my day has been, I am most in awe of the miracle of their existence, and their connection to me, when they are sleeping. It is then that I know to the depths of my being how precious and dear to me they are.

The love I feel for them shines from me in the dark.

I grew up terrified of the dark, assuming that all children were fearful of the dark spaces in their own bedrooms. It is when we sleep, when we must set down our defenses so that we may rest, that we are most vulnerable. My mother did not even need to be present in my bedroom for me to be afraid. Often I would be in that half-dream, half-awake state, frozen with fright, certain that I could hear, not only my sister's steady breathing in the bed next to mine, but another's breath, sinister and ominous.

When I could stand it no more, when I was fully awake, heart pounding wildly and convinced the monster was upon me, I would scream out in terror and inevitably my father would come to my room, flipping on the light, fully waking my groggy sister, patiently searching under the beds and in the closet for the monster whose breath I was so certain I could hear. Those cries for help in the quiet of the sleeping house occurred frequently and regularly for many years, well into my late teens.

Never did my father lose his patience with me.

Never did my mother come to rid me of the monster in the night.

My fear of the dark left me soon after I moved out of my family home. It was only many years later that I realized the extent to which my subconscious mind remained hypervigilant even while I slept, comprehending that at my core I did not feel safe, even when asleep in my own bed in my own home.

The monster that I could hear breathing under my bed was never under my bed, or even a creature I could then identify from any part of my waking, conscious life.

It is only now that I realize that the monster in the night was the parent who never came to comfort me.

Monsters followed me
into my sleep.
Because vigilance there
I could not keep.

In the darkness
Monsters roam freely.

CHAPTER TWENTY-FOUR

I am sixteen years old. Carol is one of the cool girls in school, a cheerleader who hangs out with other cool kids and drives a really nice car. Carol is coming to my house. We are not really friends, but she is mad to ride horses with me, and I am mad to have a friend who is a member of the elite popular group.

I show her around the farm, and we get the saddles and bridles out. I have already captured the two horses we will ride. They are waiting, tied to the fence, tails swishing away the summer flies, feet stamping in anticipation. Carol watches while I saddle them and fit the bridles. She does not know anything about horses except that she wants to ride.

We ride all around the fields on our farm, laughing and talking. I realize that Carol is smart and funny and a bit shy, and I find myself hoping that she likes me.

When we finish riding, Carol's jeans are full of horse hair and sweat. She asks me whether she can borrow a towel to sit on for the drive home, so she won't get her car dirty.

The day is beautiful and sunny, and we are in the front yard. My mother is standing at the open kitchen window, listening to every word. When Carol finishes asking to borrow a towel, I look at my mother through the window. She is vehemently shaking her head *no*.

What to do? We have plenty of towels. Carol's request is reasonable. I stall in my response while I steal glances at the window. My mother's head shaking becomes more and more violent. I know that if I disobey I will pay the consequences later. I also know that refusing a reasonable request will look strange and impolite to Carol.

My mind quickly does a cost analysis. There is a possibility that Carol will drive away and just think I am weird. I hope she won't tell anyone.

There is also the strong probability that lending Carol a towel will result in physical abuse.

So I tell Carol I can't lend her a towel. She is flabbergasted, promising to wash it and return it promptly, telling me that she really doesn't want to wreck her car seat and that she has nothing else to sit on. I hold steadfast in my refusal as I sneak peeks to the head in the window.

Carol finally drives away, confused and hurt at my strange response to her reasonable request.

When I finally go back into the house my mother angrily tells me that I am not to be giving away her towels or anything else in the household. When I try to explain that

Carol only wanted to borrow the towel, my mother launches into a nonsensical tirade that people are always stealing her things and that I was too stupid to realize that Carol would never have returned the towel.

Your view of the world
warped by that intruder
was at odds
with
the world I knew.

This made
no
sense.

You made
no
sense.

CHAPTER TWENTY-FIVE

One in four adults will, during some time in their life, have a mental illness.

Growing up in rural America, I had no idea of these statistics. Most people in my generation were unaware of the insidious mental illness that lived in some of their classmates' homes. We were all aware of the crazy people who were disheveled, dirty, smelly and homeless, lurching down the street, deep in loud conversations with no one. That was the only public face of mental illness where I grew up in the 60s and 70s.

It was no fault of ours that we didn't know. Treatment for mental illness was crude. People with a mental illness simply were not part of society. They were hidden away, institutionalized, forgotten. They belonged to no one. They were less than a marginalized population. People stepped carefully around the possibility of their existence, knowing that if they did not acknowledge them, they did not exist.

When you grew up with mental illness in your home, then, it is no surprise that you told no one. It was one of many deep secrets that our family kept. We never discussed it. We didn't have to. Even as children we knew that it was social suicide to acknowledge that one of those crazy people who lurched down the street talking to themselves was living in your home, and in fact, closely related to you.

Not only did we never tell anyone outside the family what was happening, we never told adult family members about what was happening either. Retribution was a powerful deterrent, one that my mother used very effectively.

Keeping this secret was hard work. The social landscape in the Midwest in the 1970s was centered around reciprocity; if you were invited to someone's house, you would go, and then invite them to come to your house a week or so later. My mother's disease made this very difficult.

I jumped at the opportunity to go to my friends' houses. I basked in the normalcy of these homes, marveled at how peaceful and fun it was. But reciprocating was difficult.

Having friends for a sleepover was risky: the secret might be revealed, as often my mother could not control herself for more than a few hours. Having friends over to play was difficult, too, and I had to gauge how the day was going before I committed to it. I was constantly alert for signs that my mother was about to lose control, which made escape plans essential. There was no telling what she would do or say if she had an outburst.

Carol and I have talked about this incident. She has never forgotten it. It stuck in Carol's mind as a bizarre response from me, something that seemed so totally out of sync with the person she knew, something so unreasonable in the circumstances, that she drove away not knowing what to think about it.

Veronica's only child, my cousin Joe, often stayed with us. He loved staying at the farm, and his greatest wish was to have siblings. Joe had to have known the secret, but he never acknowledged it. His mother, my aunt Veronica, likewise knew, as she stayed with us when my mother was acutely unwell and away in the hospital. Veronica never said a word, never acknowledged my mother's mental illness.

I was never close to my grandmother and my aunt as a child. I didn't feel as though I could be, as though that would somehow be breaching our strict rules. It was a different time, a time when people tended to mind their own business to a fault. Their role in my childhood was important, but quite limited. It is confusing to me, even now, because I love my Gram and my aunt dearly, but I only really got to know them and consciously love and appreciate them after I moved away from home. As a child I did not spend much time with them, other than the occasional sleepover and family get-togethers. Never did we discuss anything that was going on at home, our mother's strange behavior, the collateral damage that became increasing obvious as we grew older.

As a young adult I spent lots of time with my Gram, living with her on and off throughout my college years. It was only then that we were able to talk about the strangeness of my childhood, the helplessness Gram felt to say or do anything, the fear that doing so would result in her never seeing us again.

It was during these conversations that I realized that our careful pretending did not hide the serious dysfunction in our home.

Looking back on it now, I can't help but wonder if we weren't all crazy for pretending so hard that something so big and all-encompassing did not live in our house.

Like a bloody severed head
on the kitchen floor
We stepped carefully around it
Pretending it did not exist.

CHAPTER TWENTY-SIX

I am in the car with my brother and my sisters. My mother is driving us to see her parents. My father, as usual, is too busy to go. It is a boring, hour-long drive to see our grandparents, who live in the middle of nowhere.

We make this trip every few months. The five of us squabble and bicker in the back seat while my mother rides shotgun in the front. We are decades before safety belts and child restraints, and the combined energy of the five of us seems to burst out of the back seat. Every now and then my mother screams at us to shut up and drives with one hand while she tries to slap any of us within reach of her other hand. Doing so causes her to swerve and careen around, and we are tossed around in the back seat, causing even more squabbling and bickering.

My mother is an only child, so there are never cousins, uncles or aunts in attendance. Occasionally there are other dusty old relatives at these visits, but usually the only people in the house when we visit are my grandmother and grandfather.

We finally turn off the highway onto an old gravel road, then into a dirt driveway. At the end of the driveway is a small, sad house and decrepit old farm buildings with peeling paint, sagging rooftops and doors hanging awkwardly on partial, broken hinges. A dog half-heartedly approaches the car, more curious than friendly, and goes back to lying in the dirt by the side of the house before my mother even turns off the car engine.

We pile out of the car and stand together in unity, none of us wanting to go into the house first. Once we are in the house we are not allowed to play outside, or, for that matter, play at all.

My mother hisses at us to get into the house and to behave ourselves or ELSE, and we traipse up *en masse* to the weathered door. A tiny woman answers the door and we pile into the little house without any exchange of greetings.

Once we are all assembled in the front room we formally say our hellos to the woman, our grandmother. There is no hugging or any kind of physical contact exchanged at any time during the visit. My mother also formally greets her mother, also without any physical contact. We are then herded to the back of the house to an enclosed, weather-beaten porch.

There is a large hulking man sitting in a sagging, filthy, brown and gold floral chair in the corner of the porch, spitting into a spittoon, drinking out of a dirty, brown bottle. This part of the house smells like stale beer, urine, the sweat of an old man, and the rancid smell of used chewing tobacco. This is my grandfather. We repeat our formal hellos to the man, who does nothing but stare at us and grunt.

We crowd into the small kitchen, the five of us children, our mother, our grandmother, and with the old man still on the porch, we now completely fill up the small house. My grandmother, a bird-like woman not much bigger than us, scurries around, setting out strange concoctions of food for us—clear gelatin with dill pickles and pineapple chunks, strange-tasting cookies, colored, tepid water.

There are only two chairs at the kitchen table in this miniature kitchen, so we stand over the plates our grandmother has set out for us. We try to eat the peculiar food and pretend that it is delicious while my mother glares at us and makes it clear that we will pay the consequences if we do not enjoy the food her mother has gone to some trouble to make for us. I cannot look at my sister Joan or my brother John because I know we will laugh uncontrollably at the bizarre comedy in which we are starring. We have done this before, and we are adept at pretending to eat this food while pushing it under the side of the plate.

We volunteer to clean up, and when my mother, her mother, and my two youngest sisters go back into the sitting room, Joan, John and I throw the food quietly out the back door for the dog to eat while we clean up the dishes. While we are cleaning up, Joan, the comedian of the three of us, re-enacts our lunch, this time with exaggerated comic horror, her face and eyes glowing, grinning with pure joy at the prospect of eating this disgusting and bizarre food, rubbing her stomach and smacking her lips, then pretending to choke, finally crumpling to a slow, agonizing death on the floor. We clown around ferociously, but very quietly, tears streaming down our faces as we hold in our laughter. We are children, and not only do we see the craziness, but we appreciate how funny it is.

We finally have to go back to the dusty sitting room, where my mother is making forced polite conversation with her mother. We are meant to be seen and not heard, so we sit quietly. We have heard all these conversations before: there is talk of the weather; how our father is too busy to come today but really would have liked to; a cursory discussion of my grandmother's health; and then lots of boring talk about distant relatives we do not know. Most of the time there is an uncomfortable silence in the room, broken only by the loud ticking of the clock.

Never does the conversation center on the five children assembled in the room, or the drunken old man on the porch. We are props in a bizarre ritual.

We sit the entire time in anticipation of the dreaded words, "Say goodbye to your grandfather, kids." These words are bittersweet; this bizarre visit is ending but we have to once again go to the doorway of the porch and tell the creepy, old stranger, our grandfather, goodbye.

Sometimes we three oldest challenge one another to go onto the porch and get closer to my grandfather. None of us ever dared to touch him.

His only response to our chorus of goodbyes is a grunt, a spit, and a pull on the bottle.

These are my mother's parents, my grandparents. These people provided her with this sad place, her childhood home, and raised her to the adult we know as our mother.

I feel sorry for the dog as we drive away.

At least we get to leave.

All I know of you
Is what you show me of you
And what you show me of you
Is bizarre.

CHAPTER TWENTY-SEVEN

I have a strong family history of mental illness. My mother was adopted by distant relatives of her mother when she was three years old. As an adult I was able to meet, just once, two sisters of my biological grandmother. They showed me pictures of my grandmother, and told me that she was "different." They were quite unwilling to talk about what that meant. I gently continued to ask about that throughout the visit, and they said that she often did not come home at night. They mentioned that she was hospitalized from time to time at the state hospital for her "spells." When I asked questions about her spells, they were uncomfortable and would only say that she "carried on."

They remained vague and uncomfortable discussing it, but it is clear that my biological grandmother was mentally ill, and that the mental illness was likely schizophrenia. In my mother's case, both nature and nurture conspired against her odds of remaining mentally healthy.

My mother's biological mother became pregnant in her late teens by a married man in town. She had the baby, and my grandmother's parents kept the baby girl. That in itself is unusual for that time period, when unmarried pregnant girls were whisked away to a convent, out of sight, to quietly have the baby, which was then given up for adoption. The shame that attached to the woman and her family was whispered about for years thereafter. I am proud of these great-grandparents I was never able to meet, proud that they did not condone this treatment of unmarried mothers, proud that they did not force this shame upon this special, fragile daughter of theirs.

When my mother was three her grandmother died, and my grandfather, unable to raise a baby by himself, gave her to distant relatives to adopt. This childless older couple consisted of a raging alcoholic and his tiny wife who never dared to challenge him. They lived in the country, their nearest neighbor miles away. The last year or so that we went for our visits our grandmother was obviously suffering from dementia—a condition that was ignored by the adults around us in yet another strange game of real-life pretend.

I do not know what happened in that house as my mother grew up. I know that she was alone there, except for those two people. She had very few, if any, friends. I know that her alcoholic, adopted father never cared for her at all.

Looking back on these dreadful visits, I realize that my mother desperately wanted to be normal. Visiting her parents with her children was an attempt at normalcy. It was what "normal" people did. Often the only sound during those visits was the large clock on the piano and the sound of the man in the other room, spitting and drinking. The visits were always formal and uncomfortable.

On the long drive home, rather than talking to us about the strangeness of the situation, my mother would talk brightly about what a fun visit that was and how great our grandparents were. It seemed impossible that we had all just participated in the same activity. She actually seemed really happy about having been there. None of us dared tell her how awful it was for us, how we marked the time by the ticking of the clock, how we simultaneously dreaded and looked forward to telling our grandfather goodbye.

It was all so strange. As a child, it was all I knew of my mother's life before us.

Nature was against you
Daughter of your mother

Nurture was against you
Daughter of your parents

Broken flower
dropped
into
barren wasteland.

CHAPTER TWENTY-EIGHT

I learned how to be a woman from my friends, their mothers, my aunt, and my grandmother. Given this hodge-podge, and appreciating that these women did not realize the role they played in the development of my femininity, it is no wonder that I have gaps in my knowledge of women's business.

These gaps are sometimes funny, but mostly just sad. I was nineteen when my university roommate pointed out that underwear in the United States is sized radically differently than other women's clothing, which is why mine was so big on me. The changes to my body wrought by puberty, and later, pregnancy and childbirth, were confusing and shocking, but I had no one to ask, "Is this normal?"

I was hopeless at fashion, make-up, hair and nails until well into my adult life. It's not as though my mother did not set an example, but her behavior was erratic and wildly fluctuating. Like a moving target, I was unable to consistently model my femininity.

There are other, more subtle things. My first and strongest idea of what a marriage was like, and the role of the woman in a marriage, was observing the one in my house, which was neither happy nor healthy. My primary role model for all things feminine was my mother. From her I observed how a woman interacted with her husband, her children, her relatives, her neighbors. I watched her to learn how to act and react.

I entered adulthood very confused about who I was. I did not understand or particularly like women, and yet I was one. It was as though there had been a long induction process and I had missed out on it.

I was more comfortable with men than with women until I was in my thirties. I thought that women had a problem being friends with me. That was a more palatable option than the alternative, which is that perhaps the problem lay with me. I didn't trust women, and I assumed that my distrust was reasonable.

I understood men. Because I understood them, I was not afraid of them and was comfortable with them. My strong preference for the company of men led to an inconsistency in the boundaries I had with women and men. I had tall, thick, iron walls with barbed razor wire at the top for women, and a wide-open gate with streamers, balloons, and a "WELCOME!" sign for men. These strict boundaries for women meant that I had few female friends. The loose boundaries for men, coupled with my low self-esteem, led to blurring of appropriate physical, emotional, and mental intimacy.

I was not aware of my porous boundaries with men, nor how I pushed women away. I had no idea how confusing the messages were that I conveyed.

My adult relationships with my Gram and my aunt Veronica helped me to develop trust in women. Motherhood, though, was a culmination of a number of things that led me to begin to be aware of and understand my issues with both men and women. I realized that because I could not trust the most important and influential female in my life—my mother—I believed I could not trust any woman. That belief became irrational when I had a daughter—a little woman of my own.

When I became a mother, I was in a supportive, loving, (though ultimately troubled) marriage. I became very good friends with an older woman who agreed to be my daughter's grandmother—and so became a mother figure to me. And I began to see myself through the eyes of my daughter, to define myself as Briana's mother. During this time in my life I was able to finally begin to trust women, to develop appropriate boundaries and to understand how my childhood had impacted my relationships with both men and women.

I learned to be friends with women, though it was difficult for many years. I had to overcome my inherent distrust of women to do so. And I learned to develop and maintain appropriate boundaries with men. The one led naturally to the other.

I treasure my friends, men and women.

But my healing is this: I cherish my women friends and could never live without them. They have been my loving friends, my chosen sisters, my surrogate mothers, my other daughters.

I have come a long way.

From the mother the daughter learns
(theoretically at least)
The ways of a healthy woman.
How to be.
Not me.

From the world I had to unlearn
(painfully slowly)
How to be.
And redefine
me.

CHAPTER TWENTY-NINE

All of us had our own reaction to what was going on around us. We all had our own complex systems of survival.

My brother John is nearly three years older than me. I am the second oldest, then follows my sister Joan. I am four years older than Rose and eight years older than Sue.

John was rarely disciplined by my mother. He was not around the rest of us that often, working outside with my father, or in his bedroom, listening to music. John removed himself from the situation, from all of us, every opportunity he had. He shut down from us and from the situation.

As the oldest of my sisters, I felt very protective of them. Some of that arose naturally from my role as their big sister. That was enhanced by me taking care of them as a mother would, because our mother was not always able to do so. I felt a responsibility to keep them safe and to help them make their way in a world—in a home—that seemed too harsh for children. I felt better equipped to survive than I thought them to be.

By virtue of my age I had an enormous advantage over my two youngest sisters, Rose and Sue. Joan, sensitive and sweet, felt everything acutely and wrestled with her pain. Her struggles knocked her off balance and affected her ability to function.

Not me.

I managed to channel the pain that accompanied the chaos into creative outlets. I played the piano, wrote poems and stories, daydreamed. I studied hard and excelled at school. In some respects, I appeared to thrive.

Having always excelled at anything I put my mind to, I put my mind to our survival—a good thing when you need to be in survival mode. But the funny thing is that my mind, so accustomed to the struggle to survive, did not know when to stop being in survival mode. Even when I was long gone from my childhood home and that need to struggle to survive, I didn't seem to be fully alive unless I could continue to do what it seemed I did best—handle a crisis.

I was more comfortable in the chaos than the calm. I understood chaos. I knew the rules. I had an important part to play, a part I knew and understood and at which I had become very adept. I had a sense of anxiety unless I had just finished dealing with chaos, was in the midst of chaos, or could feel that chaos was impending.

I did not trust the calm. It did not feel real to me. Knowing that it was only a matter of time before the calm would end, I did not want to become intoxicated by it, relax into it. I did not understand the rules, my role. Calm was a foreign country with strange customs and a language I did not understand.

This had an enormous impact on my adult life.

I created chaos where there was none, threw problems up in front of myself, sabotaged the seemingly natural course of my life so that I could continue to play out what I had known and learned so well as a child. These were good transferable skills, and I used them to become a very good lawyer. I became skilled at quick creative lateral thinking outside the box.

My need for unrest led to what felt to me like exciting, demanding places—a career where my job was to simultaneously solve and create problems, where I had to think quickly on my feet, and in the midst of those storms, appear cool and calm, able to rationalize and persuade. It led me to a marriage to a wonderful man with multiple addictions. I looked for conflict in my personal relationships, pushing on potential weak spots until they erupted. Over and over again, when my life became quiet, I purposely stirred it up. It made me feel alive, fulfilled. *It made me feel normal*

I was good at making it look legitimate. Perhaps those closest to me knew. I certainly did not. Only once did anyone ever name it, tell me that I insisted upon making my already complex life more complicated and difficult. I know now how hard it was for him to say that to me. He must have been apprehensive about telling me, and my reaction would only have confirmed his misgivings. When he told me that I was purposely making my life more difficult, I paused, unable or unwilling to initially compre-hend what he was saying—that I was the architect of my own difficult life.

I remember still the physical sensation of an enormous, rapid uncoiling from deep within myself of denial, the panic I felt as he touched on this truth, how my brain and physical self, horrified, screamed inside myself that he was right. I remember stepping outside myself and watching my outward reaction to him, how I verbally attacked him until he backed down. My higher self knew that he was right. The rest of me was not prepared to even consider the possibility that many of the difficulties in my life were my own doing.

But the stress that resulted from the constant chaos and drama in my life manifested, as it must do. Our bodies can only handle so much before they let us know, gently at first, then more and more insistently, that stress does not just evaporate away at the end of each day. On the outside, I thrived on stress. On the inside, it was killing me.

Throughout my thirties I went to my family doctor with one stress-related physical disorder after another. My body was shouting at me that what I was doing was not working. Recognizing the problem was only a small part of the solution for me. I did not take responsibility for creating the stress in my life. I assumed that my life was more stressful than others' lives, but I also assumed that I was naturally better equipped than other mere mortals to handle it. I didn't need as much sleep as other, weaker, humans. I could juggle multiple tasks successfully and make it look easy. I excelled at everything and rarely turned away from a challenge.

Or so I thought. I finally addressed my preference for chaos because my physical body was unable to cope. Continuing to deny that I purposely made my life more difficult meant my physical self would continue to suffer and struggle and ultimately break down.

In the natural ebbs and flows of my life, there will be some stress. There will be unavoidable chaos. There will also be calm. There will be, inevitably, times of peace. I have learned, finally, to accept both the chaos and the peace. I have learned to permit the calm, to trust that it is real, to settle into it without sending it away. Soon enough it will change, and then change again. The one certainty in life is that nothing stays the same. I would have it no other way.

Did living with my mother's mental illness push me and shape me so that I had no choice but to learn this valuable lesson? If I had had a "normal" childhood, would I have ever learned this? Would I have had the need for such learning?

I choose to think that this is one of the gifts living with mental illness offered to me.

She stands steady on her feet
her voice firm and articulate
Her place in the world seemingly hers.

Why would she need any help?
Who cares what her childhood was like?
She has overcome it. She is resilient.

And then she looks down at herself
The enormous gaping hole still there.
Nobody else sees it.

It is all she can see.

CHAPTER THIRTY

I am nearly eighteen years old.

I am counting down the days to my eighteenth birthday, the day I can legally move out of our house. My father does not want me to go and is angry that I am openly making plans to move out. He forbids me to move out before I turn eighteen. We have loud arguments about his stubborn requirement that I become an adult in the eyes of the law before I leave my childhood home.

My mother's mental illness wants me out of the house faster than I am legally able to leave. This causes her to pick increasingly aggressive arguments with me and to criticize me constantly.

It is Saturday and my father and my brother are outside on the farm, working. My three sisters and I are in the house with our mother. She has had us doing chores for the past several hours.

As the day wears on, my mother's rage increases, until finally she is physically following me around the house, berating me. I cannot get away from her. Eventually she shoves me down onto the floor on my back, screaming at me. She sits on my chest, straddling my arms to pin me down. I feel pressure on my chest. I hear THUMP THUMP THUMP in my ears. I panic as I struggle to breathe, try to get her off me, pushing against her with all my might, the ineffectiveness only increasing my panic and using up my breath. I try to scream, but I do not have enough air to make much than a whimper.

Then my mother puts her hands around my throat and begins to squeeze. I look up and my three sisters are standing around us, looking down at me with helpless horror in their eyes. I can see and hear them screaming at her to stop. They are crying, powerless. They are afraid.

I become very calm. I am acutely aware of each and every detail: the pain and pressure on my throat, the feeling that my chest is going to explode, the small black spots in my vision. I am keenly able to hear each and every sound: my sisters' crying, my mother's quick breaths, my sister Joan's voice as though from far away, begging my mother to stop. I feel the warmth of my mother's breath in my face, smell the coffee she has been drinking all day. I see my mother's face and the far-away look in her eyes, and I know that my mother is not doing this but the intruder has completely taken over.

I separate from my body and float above, watching from a safe place. I know that my life is ending, and I am calm and somewhat relieved.

I hope that my sisters will not be traumatized for the rest of their lives by watching this, helpless to stop it. I want them to know that there is nothing they can do, that this is a terrible thing to see, that I am so sorry that they are witnessing this. I will these thoughts to all three of them in turn, everything going in slow motion, the universe accommodating without question my need to make sure my sisters have my reassurances, my last task as their big sister and substitute mother.

I am not afraid. I am accepting and feel soft and peaceful.

And then I hear the kitchen door open, a pause, the soft curse of my brother, the rush of his feet across the floor, the grunt as he pulls my mother off me.

I lie there on the floor as my mother lies a few feet away from me where my brother has dragged her. Neither of us moves or speaks. My sisters are crying as my brother repeatedly asks my mother what she is doing. She is silent and still.

Joan helps me get up, helps me out the door, and takes me to the hayloft in the barn where she sits with her arm around me in the soft sweetness, safely away from my mother. There is nothing to be said.

That night my mother, puzzled about why my voice is raspy, asks what is wrong with me and why I am ignoring her. The intruder in our home has retreated for the moment, and my mother has forgotten what she did to me, the murderous thoughts that screamed at her now lying dormant and silent in her mind. I tell her and she denies it, though I can see that she is confused.

When my sisters confirm what I tell her, she goes to her room and shuts the door. I do not see her again for the rest of that day, or the next.

She knew not
what she did.

CHAPTER THIRTY-ONE

A side from my experiences with the intruder in my home, growing up on a farm was a wonderful experience for me. I developed an enormous appreciation for animals, as they were a big part of our lives. The births and deaths of the many creatures on our farm did not go unnoticed by us. One of the animal groups that we children monitored endlessly was our cat population. Of the many cats I grew up with, I remember a few of them as standouts.

One such cat was a female we named Dusty because of her wispy grey coat. I remember Dusty because Dusty was really unusual.

Every time Dusty gave birth to kittens, she ate them.

It was horrifying.

Something was wrong with Dusty. Some part of her hardwiring received jumbled signals, signals which overrode the instincts she carried deep within herself. Perhaps mental illness lived within Dusty, too, whispered in her ear that this flesh of her flesh must die, screamed that the one who gave these little ones life must also take that life away.

Sometimes mothers harm, and even kill, their children. Doing so overrides all instinct. I feel deep sympathy for these women, many of whom are profoundly damaged. I am sad when people demand harsh punishment for the incomprehensible crimes of these women. I realize that my childhood allows me to have compassion for these women, that I have some first-hand comprehension of the incomprehensible.

The home I grew up in was a violent place. In addition to the physical and verbal abuse by my mother, we children often responded with violence to one another when the stress became unbearable. This was natural; we had observed this all of our lives. It seems bizarre to me now that we could draw together so closely and yet push back against each other so violently.

My father's presence in the house meant a reprieve from physical violence. Never did I see my father strike anyone; never did I fear that my father would physically harm me or my siblings. The problem was that my father was rarely in the house. He never moved away or stayed out all night, but he worked both a fulltime job and was a fulltime farmer.

I moved out on my eighteenth birthday, the very first moment I was legally able to do so. I still had three months before I would graduate from high school. Moving out gutted my father. He tried to talk me out of it, but there was no way I was staying; I was desperate to go. I was afraid I would not survive if I stayed.

My mother's behaviors had become increasingly bizarre and violent. She fixated on me, relating incredible stories about my plots to murder her, accused me of an incestuous relationship with my father, told me she knew all about my evil influence over my sisters.

When I stood at the kitchen sink washing dinner dishes at night, the dark window in front of me a mirror, she would walk behind me, arm raised up with a knife as though to stab me. I was afraid of her.

It wasn't just her verbal and mental attacks on me. Her physical attacks increased in intensity and frequency. She could not help herself, working herself into a frenzy with her irrational thought process, and then physically acting on her thoughts. I did not fight back, never lifting a hand against her, though I often argued with her verbally.

One of the lingering effects of the violence in my house is my reaction to witnessing violence. I am horrified at watching violence. It fills me with fear and helplessness. If I watch a violent scene in a movie, I can feel the violence occurring to me, acutely and vividly. There is no filter through which the violence travels, no reality check that the violence is not real. It feels real to me, and it feels like it is happening to me.

My revulsion to violence as a young girl caused me to do something that makes very little sense. When my mother's illness demanded that she lash out physically, I often stepped in and deflected her away from my sisters. Sometimes her refocus onto me caused her to hurt me. It was a risk I was willing to take. I did not do this because I was trying to protect them; I did this for a very selfish reason: I could not stand to watch the violence. I could not even stand to imagine it happening. I preferred to have it happen to me. It was better than witnessing it, helpless to do anything. It was preferable to running away from it while its potential played over and over in my head. And it was preferable to seeing the hurt of my little sisters later.

On New Year's Eve, 1980, I graphed 79 boxes on a big piece of construction paper and filled them in with numbers in reverse chronological order. This was a countdown to my eighteenth birthday, when I could legally move away.

But my mother's mental illness sensed that I was fleeing. I believe now that my mother must have been terribly conflicted those last few months before my eighteenth birthday. She surely understood why I counted the days to my freedom. In the tiny portions of my mother's mind that were not inhabited by her mental illness, she would have mourned driving her daughter away, would have realized the part she played in the desire of this human being to get away from her.

I realize now that my mother was in an acute phase of illness during those months. Stress and change were precipitators for flare-ups. All the behaviors escalated—the paranoia, the verbal abuse, the violence.

My emancipation nearly did not happen.

Had my brother not come in when he did, there is no doubt that I would not have survived. At a conscious level, where the collateral damage had blown away any semblance of perspective and normalcy, *I thought that what happened that day was within the realm of normal behavior for our family.*

This is important. It was normal for us. My death at the hands of my own mother was a reasonably foreseeable outcome to what was occurring in our household.

Dusty always ate her kittens. That was normal for Dusty.

My mother wanted to kill me. That was normal for my mother.

Fighting a demon
under the best of circumstances
takes courage and strength.

Fighting a demon
inside your head
utterly alone
with no weapons
no help
the fight relentless
the stakes not negotiable...

Well.

Let's just say
Battles are sometimes lost.

CHAPTER THIRTY-TWO

One month before my daughter was born, my husband's mother died. My mother was completely out of my life and had been so for years. Before my daughter was born, I asked my good friend Teri to be my daughter Briana's grandmother. I did not want her to miss out on having a grandmother, a relationship that had been, for me, the most unconditional love I had ever known.

Teri has been a fantastic grandmother for my children, and I will always be grateful to her for stepping forward and gracefully filling that important role.

When Briana was seven, she realized that Teri was not actually my mother. It was then that I told her the parts of my story fit to tell a seven-year-old. She was very curious about what my mother looked like, what she sounded like, what she was like. Finally, one day she asked whether she could meet her. My son joined in the request, curious to meet the mother of his mother.

I would have preferred that she had asked me for a kidney, or part of my liver, perhaps one of my eyes. I was miserable at the thought of making contact with my mother. But my beautiful daughter was gently insistent, and I could understand her curiosity. I had always wanted to meet my biological grandparents.

I finally called my mother. She didn't know who I was at first. She was cold, unresponsive. As I nervously explained that the kids wanted to meet her, she was very quiet.

After a long silence, she agreed.

We agreed to meet at the shopping mall in the town near where I grew up. The children were very excited about the visit, and I instructed them not to talk about me, nor the past. They were puzzled: of course they wanted to ask her about me, and our family. In anticipation of the visit we decided to put together photo albums of their lives, with pictures of their pets, their friends, trips they had been on, and they could use the photos to show her and tell her about those things.

They told me that they each wanted to give her a gift as well, reminding me, at my surprised reaction, that she IS their grandmother.

Jamie chose a teapot and cup, and Briana chose a stuffed animal. They wrapped up their gifts, packed their photo albums, and we drove to the shopping center for the meeting.

I drove that twenty-minute drive from my father's house to the shopping mall with a sick feeling in my stomach. Nearly twenty years had passed since I last had a conversation with my mother, but the thought of even seeing her again was daunting.

We sat in the café area of the mall, waiting.

"What does she look like?" the children kept asking with excitement.

"Do you think you'll recognize her?"

And, in fact, I did not. I have always been told that I look exactly like my mother, and in some photos, even I can see our physical resemblance. So I was curious, wondering if this woman would be the physical picture of the future me, and if so, what that future me would look like. But I did not recognize the small, grey-haired, slightly stooped woman who looked older than her 63 years. I recognized her second husband, flagging him down and guiding him to the table. I could not look at the woman who accompanied him.

We made awkward introductions, and then I excused myself, telling them that I would be back in forty-five minutes. I knew that my mother would not relax with my children if I sat there. So I went into a music store where I could look out the window behind my mother to keep an eye on things. I was shaking inside as I watched them proudly start to tell their stories, showing her the photo albums they'd carefully put together just for this visit. I watched as their enthusiasm waned with the lack of reaction.

After forty-five minutes I made my way back to the table and sat down quietly as my son was telling his story. My daughter kept looking back and forth at the face of this stranger and the face of her mother. I could see that she was trying to put it all together. I carefully avoided looking at my mother, listening intently to the story Jamie was telling.

And then my mother stood up abruptly. The visit was over, she announced. She had chores to do and they needed to go. She gathered up her gifts and turned and walked away. Her husband followed her, head down.

She did not say goodbye. She did not tell my children it was a pleasure to meet them. She did not thank them for the gifts they had given her. She did not raise the possibility of ever seeing them again. She simply stood up, announced she was leaving, and walked away.

My children were stunned. My daughter, in particular, had never known anything but unconditional love from the adults in her life. Even my son, who lived in foster homes for the first few years of his life until I adopted him, had never experienced this kind of bizarre behavior.

I asked them how they felt the visit had gone. "It was good," they both said, without any enthusiasm. We continued to make small talk. I could see that the children were still trying to sort it all out. Finally my daughter burst out, "I can't believe she was ever mean to you!" That was the catalyst for a true debriefing. They agreed that she was too small and old for them to contemplate that she was capable of being "mean" to her children. They talked about how she appeared to be listening, but did not respond to their stories. She did not react, but sat, with a forced smile on her face, nodding occasionally. They agreed that it was "weird" that she just suddenly stood up and walked away.

I offered to set up another meeting if they wanted to do so. My daughter contemplated this possibility for a moment, then said, "No, mommy, I just wanted to see what she's like. I don't need to see her again." My son agreed.

As we sat and talked that day, I watched as they eventually normalized what had happened. They agreed that I look a lot like my mother, which I denied with comic exaggerated horror. On the drive home they told me again, with glee, that I look just like her, and that has been the only residue from that visit—from time to time, to tease me, they will remind me that I look just like my mother.

Grandmother:
Mother of my mother
twice my mother.
And yet
Not.

CHAPTER THIRTY-THREE

I grew up knowing that my mother would have been a famous singer were it not for the fact that she married my father and had five children that she never wanted. How did I know this? She told us so. Many times.

When the loud strains of Mantovani began from the record player, that was a signal to us kids: the famous singer was in the house. The famous singer might be staying with us a few hours or a few days, but the famous singer's presence in the house meant:

1. No meals. Famous singers did not have to cook for anyone. In fact, they had people cooking just for them.

2. No housework. Famous singers did not do housework.

3. No getting us up and off to school. Famous singers need their sleep.

4. Lots and lots of loud singing. Because that's what famous singers do.

5. The "lecture."

The lecture consisted of her telling us repeatedly and with great drama that "if only" she hadn't gotten married and had all these children she never wanted, she would have been a famous singer. We heard all about the talent of this famous singer, the likes of which had no equal and had never been seen before in the history of the world. The longer the visit by the famous singer, the more aggressive and angry the lecture, and if the famous singer stayed in the house long enough, the lecture culminated in physical abuse.

It was not until I was a teenager that it dawned on me that the chances of my mother becoming a famous singer would have been abysmal under the best of circumstances. The most glaring problem was that she could not sing.

But as a child I felt sorry for my mother and her unrequited dream. I also felt incredibly guilty. Were it not for my existence, my mother would be happy. Clearly, she was extremely unhappy. Clearly, it was my fault.

That kind of guilt could not help but affect how I viewed myself and my place in the world.

As suddenly as she had come for a visit, the famous singer would leave.

And life would get back to normal. Sort of. It's all so relative, isn't it?

*I need to remind myself
that I am here in this world legitimately,
that my existence
is not responsible for anyone's failures or successes,
that I can take up space,
make noise,
and be fully present in this life.*

CHAPTER THIRTY-FOUR

I am fourteen years old. I get on my bicycle and ride, fast as I can, my legs pumping furiously, my feet pushing down hard on the pedals. I am fleeing the intruder in my home who insists that my mother hurt me. I must get away, and fast.

I know where I am going, as I go to this place often, and many times under these circumstances. It is six miles away, across gravel roads and hills, but I could go there with my eyes closed. It is the home of my best friend. More importantly to me on these occasions, it is the home of the mother of my best friend.

I bike hard, sweating, crying. When I pull up to the house I set the bike down on the porch. I can hear the sounds of a large, happy family eating dinner, and I ease through the screen door, afraid to look up from my shoes.

Maureen quietly sets another plate and silverware and pulls a chair up to the table next to my best friend. She goes to the door and takes my shoulders, gently herding me to the table. Her husband glances at me and continues to eat, obviously displeased at this interruption. Her eight children look at me and then at their mother, who gracefully continues the dinner conversation without missing a beat as she dishes me up a meal. My best friend, who knows only that I have trouble with my mother and that she is rarely invited to my house, nudges me with her elbow and smiles at me.

I know that Maureen will always make space for me at this table. I know that she will not ask lots of questions, but will look at me with the sympathy of knowing that something is terribly wrong. I know, too, that she will always be kind to me.

I know that she will take me aside and softly ask me if I am okay, and I will always reply that I am, even when I am not.

The answer is not as important as the question.

If it is too dark for me to safely ride my bicycle home, she will load the bicycle in the back of the station wagon and drive me to just down the road from my home so that I can ride the bike for the last little way.

I am twelve years old. I love the school library and I am here, lost in the stacks of books, trying to make myself feel better by losing myself in a story. I come here often when I am upset, sometimes crying quietly as I sit on the floor hidden by walls of books, other times pushing my need to cry into desperately losing myself in a book. I don't want anyone to see me when I am upset, but sometimes the need to cry is as strong as the need to throw up when I am sick. I don't even always know why I am crying.

Mrs. Rodd, the librarian, is always kind to me, and stopped asking me what was wrong after the first few times she saw me with my wet, red eyes. Each time in response to her gentle inquiries I could only stare at the floor and will myself to stop it.

Mrs. Rodd always makes a point of greeting me, setting aside new books for me to read and taking the time to talk to me. She talks to me like an adult, tells me she has never seen anyone read as much as me, that I am intelligent, that I am wonderful.

Doing so makes me glow with happy embarrassment.

I am seventeen years old. I am at my friend Sheila's house. I am here to ask her mother's permission to move into their house in a few weeks when I turn eighteen. I have tried to find a place to rent, but I am still in high school and cannot afford a place of my own. Sheila said that her mom might be open to me living with them and paying a bit for room and board.

Sheila's mom Karen is sitting at the table smoking a cigarette and reading a magazine as I nervously approach her. I have known Karen for many years, having seen her in church and at school events, but rarely have I spoken to her at length about anything.

Karen asks me only one time why I need a place to stay, and does not press me when I tell her that I just cannot live at home anymore. She nods her head and seems to understand that these are the only words I can find to explain my situation.

Karen is kind to me, and not only agrees that I can stay with them, but treats me as a member of the family.

Karen tells me years later that I was like a wounded puppy looking for a safe place to stay.

I am seventeen years old. My family is at its lowest point ever. I am struggling. One of my teachers, Mr. Shrupp, takes me aside after class and asks me what is wrong. He points out that I have always been a straight A student and never had a problem getting my homework done, but I have been slipping. He is not accusatory, but kind in his questions, his concern for me genuine.

He asks whether it has something to do with things at home and I can only nod while struggling to hold back my tears.

He does not press me for information, but asks how he can help. His offer of help makes some of my tears slide out of my eyes and I cannot speak. I am embarrassed that Mr. Shrupp sees me crying like a baby.

Mr. Shrupp tells me that whatever is happening he wants me to remember that he is here to help in any way that he can, that he cares about me and that he has always known me to be a good, kind person. He tells me that I am brave and strong and that even brave, strong people sometimes struggle with big things they cannot do much about.

I so want to tell him about what is happening, but I know that I cannot.

Mr. Shrupp goes out of his way to greet me and talk to me during the remainder of that, my final semester of high school.

One of the high school faculty members told me years later that the faculty and staff knew that something was terribly wrong in our home, but nobody knew what to do.

You saved me
whether you knew it
or not.

I am so grateful
to each of you.

CHAPTER THIRTY-FIVE

Maureen, Mrs. Rodd, Karen, Mr. Shrupp. These are some of the lifelines of my childhood. Without these lifelines I have no doubt that the end result of my childhood would be radically different. These lifelines allowed me to hang on, verified that I was struggling and that my struggle was real, provided me with adults who saw me for who I was, and in that, acknowledged that I was a good person of value. Each of them gave me what help they could, knowing that they could not fix the Gordian knot of my childhood home.

Each of them showed me compassion. They did not interrogate me but provided me with the space necessary to accommodate the intruder in my home. I was able to rely upon and trust these adults, something I was not able to do with my parents, whose primary responsibility was to the intruder in our home.

The memory of these lifelines, even all these years later, causes me to feel very emotional and deeply grateful.

What I have realized is that to thrive, every child needs lifelines outside her parents, but children living with parental mental illness need lifelines to survive. Feeling safe, feeling valued, being seen as an individual with unique gifts, being heard—this is what adults in healthy homes provide to children. I am fortunate that I was able to connect with adults who were able to provide me with these things, even if that provision was not constant. It was, however, consistent, and I was able to rely upon it.

Mitakuye Oyasin is an expression from the Lakota people of North America. The phrase is a prayer of interconnectedness to all other people and all life forms, an affirmation that we are all connected, one to another. We are all one. When one of us feels pain, we all feel pain. When one of us helps another, we are simultaneously helpers and helped.

Mitakuye Oyasin tells me that I am not alone.

Maureen, Mrs. Rodd, Karen, Mr. Shrupp, and other adults throughout my childhood, adolescence and adulthood showed me that I was not alone.

My lifelines let me know that I mattered, that they cared about me, that I was a valuable and valued person. It was not enough to counter what I was experiencing at home, but it was enough to plant the seeds of my self-worth.

The child
abandoned in a wasteland
dying of thirst
starving.

Needs so much less
appreciates so much more
the small crumbs and little sips
of
compassion and humanity
than one fully nourished.

CHAPTER THIRTY-SIX

My son called me crazy today. He is a teenage boy, trying to navigate his way through a world that is often confusing and limiting. As the adult in the house, I represent to him what is wrong with the world, and at some level, he holds me responsible. And when I place boundaries on him, as I must to keep him safe, to balance the child that he still is with the adult he is so anxious to become, he loses his temper with me. When I get tired of arguing with him, as inevitably occurs, I simply stop explaining my decisions to him.

Like any child, he knows which buttons to push.

We all have them, our own personal flashpoints, words that cut to the quick so that the resulting hurt becomes paralyzing. And just for a moment or two, in the wake of that pain, before our brain is able to kick in and reason with our heart, we are laid low.

No dummy, my son, he knows what my flashpoints are. And when he wants me to feel hurt, or angry, or frustrated, he unhesitatingly slings words my way that he knows will have the desired effect. It is normal teenage behavior.

So calling me crazy from time to time is normal.

My reaction to it is not.

I panic. Anxiety swells from somewhere deep inside me, threatening to burst through my skin. And though I know I am most definitely not crazy, that knowledge is snow melting on a red-hot grill, evaporating as quickly as I can think it. So powerful are those accusatory words that I go right into a fight/flight response.

My greatest fear is that I will develop a mental illness. It is not an irrational fear; many mental illnesses have a genetic link. I saw what it did to my mother, to my sister, to the rest of us.

The depression that I developed as an infant never left me. I have come to realize that it is situational depression, but because the situation in which it developed and continued to reside went on and on, it is now a part of me, just like my brown eyes and my curly hair. And when my life becomes difficult, I rebound back into that dark space.

It is not as though anyone would ever know. I am a master at smiling when I feel like weeping, working and taking care of my children when I feel like curling up in the fetal position in a corner of my home. I keep my depression at bay much of the time, but it is always there, lurking in the corners of my brain, waiting to visit me and take me down into the well of hopelessness. I've likened it to a shadowy ghost, one whose image you can just see if you turn very quickly. There it is, at the edge of your vision, then gone again, but not gone far.

Much of the struggle I've had with my depression has been by myself. It was not until I had my daughter at the age of thirty that I finally succumbed and asked for help. In a failing marriage, with a tiny daughter to care for by myself, a demanding career, and the effects of post-partum depression, I went lower into that dark place than I ever have before. The one thing that cheered me up was the thought of ending it all. It made perfect sense to me. I was unable to feel or hope, yet I was in excruciating pain. I could not sleep, I had no appetite, I could not concentrate, but somehow I had to force myself to soldier on. It was all too much.

It was during this dark time that I saw my family doctor for a post-partum follow up. She was a very kind woman, and I trusted her. She asked me several questions, and we talked about my alarming weight loss, my inability to sleep, my loss of appetite, my fatigue. And then she said the words that caused panic to well up from deep inside of myself.

"You're suffering from depression," she said carefully. "I'd like to put you on medication to help level you off a bit. You'll also need to see a therapist."

I was devastated. The very thing I feared the most had arrived in my life—mental illness. In my mind it was only a matter of time before I turned into my mother. So I did the only thing that made sense.

I refused to listen. I left her that day, shaking inside, alarm bells blaring through all conscious thought, knowing that taking medication would cement it—that I was mentally ill. If I did not take the medication, I could not be mentally ill. It made perfect sense to me.

"I'm here if you want to talk to me, Cate, or if you change your mind," she said as she put her arm around me at the doorway of the examination room.

It was those words I remembered a month later as I sat in my office at work, door shut, staring out the window, tears streaming down my face, unable to function. I could not kill myself because I could not leave my beautiful baby. It seemed supremely selfish to continue to contemplate it.

So I picked up the phone and called my doctor.

I realized later that taking anti-depressants for that period of time in my life saved my life. I realized as well that it did not mean that I was my mother.

It did not mean that I suffered from a psychotic illness.

It did not mean that anything was "wrong" with me.

It also gave me great insight into what depression is all about for me. When my life starts to feel as though it is out of control, when I don't take care of myself, when I don't have things to look forward to, that's when my old companion Depression comes to find me.

Depression barges in when I feel like I felt when I was growing up.

Having insight into my depression is liberating. It allows me to take care of myself in such a way as to avoid depression coming, and if it does come, my insight is very helpful in managing it. It has helped me to remain mentally healthy for more than twenty years. When I feel my old companion Depression coming around, I am able to do things to ensure that I do not slide down into that dark place, because I know that at a certain point, I can no longer control the slide if I begin.

I'm lucky. Many people with a mental illness are not afforded the gift of insight, or even much of a warning. That's one of the cruelties of psychotic mental illness coupled with paranoia. Like the perfect booby-trap of the mind, any insight is explained away by the paranoia.

Sometimes a person's pancreas breaks down and that person can no longer make insulin. Diabetics have to be very conscientious and vigilant about the things that affect their physical health.

I have to be conscientious and vigilant about the things that affect my mental health.

Imagine what would happen if a diabetic had no insight into why she felt sick and shaky and fell into comas periodically? Imagine the loss of control she would experience, the lack of cause and effect, the chaos.

I imagine that's how it must have felt for my mother.

The black dog found me as a baby-
chased me all my life
always watching
always waiting
sometimes dragging me into the shadows.

And when my baby girl was born
that black dog
caught me
and dragged me
deep deep deep into that darkness.

I wanted to leave the world,
get away from that painful place.

I was terrified that my DNA was flawed-
that I was broken.

But I knew the only way I was leaving my baby girl
was kicking and screaming.

So I kicked and screamed my way out of that dark place
and sent the black dog away.

Figured out too
that I wasn't broken after all.

That damn dog
 still skulks around me
and sometimes gets close
but I am vigilant.

CHAPTER THIRTY-SEVEN

My youngest sister and her toddler recently stayed a few nights with my mother in her little house. My mother, unable to handle the added stress of these two houseguests, particularly the toddler, told my sister to make other arrangements. They had an argument, during the course of which my sister asked my mother how in the world she handled five children, when clearly she could not handle even one. My mother replied, "I never had to. Your sister Cate took care of you all."

Two things surprised me: that my mother acknowledged this, and that my sister would tell me this.

As I entered my adult years, I did not want children of my own. I had already done all the work of a mother—diapers and bottles and bathing small bodies and laundry and cooking and cleaning for a houseful of people. It wasn't much fun, and I felt overwhelmed with being the *de facto* mother in a house that often didn't have one. Looking back now I realize that in filling that role I gave up my most important role: that of simply, but importantly, being a child.

Childhood is feeling secure, loved and cared for, responsibility only easing in with impending adulthood. Childhood is discovering who you are, what makes you special and unique and wonderful. Childhood is having adults upon whom to learn to model yourself. Childhood is not worrying about how you will survive. Childhood is stability, knowing what the rules are, knowing that someone who is in charge of you has the ability to accept that responsibility and knows what they're doing, and why.

I did not feel secure, loved, and cared for. I was not carefree. I discovered, through the warped lenses of my mother's eyes, that I was a person who was unlovable. I did not feel special, unique, or wonderful. I worried constantly, not only about how I would survive, but how my family was going to survive. My childhood was anything but stable.

Besides having already been a mother to my sisters, a job I didn't think was all that much fun, there were two other, bigger reasons that I did not want children of my own: 1) I was afraid I would be the same type of mother to them as my mother had been to me, and 2) I was afraid that I did not know how to be a good mom.

Though these sound the same, they are markedly different:

Not only was I afraid that I would be just like her, but even assuming that didn't happen, the default model wasn't any better. My only model for motherhood was deeply and fundamentally flawed. How would I know what to do, how to be a good mom?

Our family was in a fight for survival all the time. My mother could not assume responsibility for her five children. She did not care for us, protect us, teach us how to make our way in the world. She did not make us feel safe or loved, special or important. Sometimes she harmed us. Her mental illness made demands upon my mother, demands that that were at odds with responsible and loving mothering. And what my mother's mental illness wanted, her mental illness usually got.

Her responsibilities fell to me. I was never asked if I would accept them, responsibilities that could be a heavy burden on the shoulders of an adult, an impossibly onerous burden on the small shoulders of a child. I was the logical choice to fulfill those duties. And because I was a child when those duties became mine to fulfill, I never thought I had an option to refuse them.

I took on those additional responsibilities and I took them seriously. I had incentives to do them well.

I always hoped that if the house was clean enough, if the meal was good enough, if I did well at school, if my siblings' homework was done and done right, perhaps my mother would love me. Her stinging criticism confirmed what I already suspected: that I wasn't good enough, that I did not merit her approval and her love. And rather than giving up, her rebukes only spurred me on to try harder, do better, be better. I did not know, could not know, that it was her mental illness that whispered to my mother that nothing I ever did was good enough.

Did my personality dictate how I performed my roles, or did those roles play a big role in the evolution of my personality? I do not know. I am grateful for my strong work ethic. I take great satisfaction in doing a job well. I have healed enough to recognize when my work is well done, and, more importantly, to recognize if criticism of me or my work is meritorious or not. If living with my mother's mental illness steered me in that direction, then I will accept that as one positive side effect of my childhood.

There was the added incentive of pretending to the world that all was well, that my mother was fulfilling her role, that our family was "normal." This was a powerful incentive, one that could mean the difference between social acceptance and stigmatism.

My mother was not able to fulfill her role. She was unable to be our mom. She drifted in and out of the role as her disease dictated. Her role fell to me.

Babies had to be fed. Diapers had to be changed. Laundry had to be done. Breakfast, lunch, and dinner had to be prepared. The house had to be cleaned constantly. It seemed there was no end of work for me to do in that house while I was growing up.

But because she floated in and out of her varying ability to do her job, my responsibilities fluctuated from day to day. And so I learned to be very flexible, to adopt structure when I needed to and discard it without notice. I learned to flow with the erratic nature of the illness that gripped my mother, gripped our household and our lives. This flexibility and ability to easily adopt and discard structure are extremely useful transferrable skills, gifts from my difficult childhood.

Many children are placed in the position of caring for members of their family. I know about children who are carers of their parents because of a multitude of reasons—physical disability, mental disability, mental illness. When I hear about these amazing children, I am in awe. Through all of the work I did running the household of seven people, never once did I actually care for my mother.

I could not have brought myself to do so. Bad enough she left me with all her work and responsibilities. Bad enough my childhood was pushed to the side and then left behind to make way for her mental illness. Bad enough that her illness told me I never did enough, well enough, for me to merit her approval or her love. Bad enough that she and her illness wreaked havoc in our home every day.

So to those children who cared for their parents under these circumstances—good for you. You did what I simply could not do. I admire you immensely.

And for those children who simply cannot or did not, I say this—good for you, too. And I add a warm, loving hug.

It's okay. You did the best you could.

I learned (from my mother) how not to be a mom
And so I got to be the mom I wished for but didn't have.
I learned (from my children) how to be a child
And so I experienced the childhood I wished for but didn't have.

CHAPTER THIRTY-EIGHT

Dear Sue,

As you know, we are having significant trouble getting along with each other. It is not good for either of us to constantly be at odds with one another.

We had a very dysfunctional family, something I am working hard to overcome. The issues and patterns from that time period seem to be motivating much of this. The depth and breadth of your anger toward me is increasing.

I realize that I play a part in this problem. When you are so angry with me, as you often are, I find it very difficult to simply swallow that and walk away, or pretend I don't notice how rude and abrupt you are to me. Most times I have no idea what I have done, or failed to do, to invoke your anger. Many times you treat me as an acquaintance, or an annoyance and an interruption in your busy day/life.

I am very sad about this. We have had many good times. Whatever else you think about me, I have tried very hard, and I have had good intentions. I'm not sure what happened to change our relationship, but it probably doesn't matter. This is the way it is, this is the way it has been for some time, and as long as we both continue along our respective paths, I don't believe things will change.

I continue to believe that we need help to overcome our past. Each of us walked away from that situation with different scars that barely cover our pain. I am a constant reminder to you of that. I'm truly sorry.

I think we should take an indefinite break from each other. You are my sister and I will always love you, but I cannot continue the way things have been. At some level, this will probably be a relief for you.

I truly wish the very best for you, Sue.

Love always, Cate

(Letter to my youngest sister, June 2008)

CHAPTER THIRTY-NINE

The consequences of my mother's severe mental illness did not stop with our childhood. Nor did those effects impact only my relationship with my mother. It is now, as adults, that the impact of my mother's mental illness on my relationships with my siblings is most obvious. It is these sibling relationships for which I feel the most acute loss and sorrow.

Most families have their own family traditions, often involving birthdays, holidays, daily and weekly life, shared spirituality. It is some of the glue that binds families together. We had family traditions too, but our family traditions were rarely positive and happy. Holidays were obligatory and forced. Because holidays deviated from routine, holidays were difficult for my mother and usually resulted in a flare-up of her symptoms. Compounding that was my mother's own difficult history around these family traditions. It was during these times that the voices in her head were often the loudest and most demanding.

Celebrations were usually preceded by or followed with spikes in my mother's mental illness. It felt to me as though we were going through the motions to maintain some semblance of normalcy. Always we walked on eggshells, waiting for the inevitable manifestation of my mother's inability to handle what was happening.

Mealtimes were often miserable. My father joked that our supper menu was usually hot tongue and cold shoulder. My mother was often either silent and sullen for reasons unknown to us, or angry and loudly critical about minor things or things that made no sense. I remember my father trying to make mealtimes happy and light, but by the time I was in my mid-teens my father had given up trying.

We went to weekly church service as a family, where the glaring hypocrisy of our life was reinforced. For an hour we intoned prayers and heard readings about honoring one another and loving one another, following the golden rule, the importance of family and community. My mother's mental illness did not listen or pray. The peaceful, loving utopia religion preached to me week after week seemed like an impossibility in our lives. Always, we returned to the inevitability of my mother's mental illness.

Intuitively it would seem that for us siblings our shared experience and memories would bind us and make us close. But our childhood memories of holidays, celebrations, daily and weekly rituals are upsetting. The glue of our family relationships, the way that we are connected, is painful. Seeing one another reminds us of that painful childhood and those excruciating memories, so we have tended to avoid one another.

My siblings and I have another bond: we all experienced the same traumatic childhood home, often with only each other to understand and appreciate the difficulty of what we were going through. But we experienced that traumatic childhood home as individuals trying—sometimes competing—to survive, which was complicated by my mother's severe mental illness.

My mother discriminated in her treatment of us depending upon our birth rank, the role we played in that dysfunctional family, our reaction to her behaviors, our personalities and coping mechanisms, our own innate sense of our selves. Her treatment of each of us might well have also been based on factors over which we had no knowledge or control—how sick she was with each pregnancy, what real or imagined difficulties we presented to her as infants and small children, who we may have reminded her of. That discrimination led to complex sibling relationships that have only grown more complex with the passage of time.

Each of us have dealt with our childhood differently, manifested the collateral damage in our own specific way. We have, each of us, emerged with issues around control, abandonment, shame, abuse, our sense of being loveable, our sense of our self. At least one of my sisters has severe mental illness, and more than one of us suffers from depression and other mental illness. The sense of hopelessness, helplessness, chaos and instability that marked our childhood has followed us all our lives. The trauma of our childhood did not melt away when we emancipated to adults.

And because we are five separate individuals we have different levels of personal insight into how our childhood has manifested in our lives. We have worked to heal—or not heal—those manifestations. The one marked difference between my siblings who continue to openly manifest their wounding and those who do not is this: understanding the role their childhood played in their adult behaviors and taking responsibility now for those adult behaviors. As adults it is pointless to continue to "blame" our parents (or each other) for the dysfunction in our lives.

We all played a part in maintaining our secret and pretending that our family was normal. My siblings and I all had a role we played in that highly dysfunctional home. As adults we tend to return to those roles when we are together. Most people, whether they grew up with a mental illness or not, would agree that when they are with their family they tend to naturally fall back into the roles they had when they were growing up.

While I have a unique relationship with each of my siblings, the common denominator is that those relationships remain very tenuous and difficult, even all these years later. Interactions with my siblings are very difficult because our actions and words are viewed through the distorted lenses of our childhood and the parts we played in our dysfunctional home. Seeing one another tends to bring back our shared childhood. Most of the time this aversion to one another is not conscious.

Our relationships with one another were never allowed to naturally develop in a healthy way, bombarded as we were by the collateral damage of my mother's severe mental illness.

I care deeply about my siblings. But the role forced upon me as their substitute mother created a warped relationship with each of them. I am deeply hurt when they accuse me of not caring about them when a big part of my life centered around caring, not only about them, but for them. I have never been able to stop feeling a maternal responsibility for them. I would never knowingly hurt them. I would do anything for them.

It has been painful for me to realize that they do not feel the same way about me. The resulting sense of loss—of my dream of having four close, supportive siblings—has been extremely difficult. I have come to realize that it is my issue to work out rather than theirs. I am still struggling with this.

Our childhood roles are hard to shake. I will always be the eldest sister and de facto mother to my siblings, with all the trappings of those complicated roles from all those years ago. It is difficult for them to view me in any other light, to see me as an adult, to stop blaming me for being a less-than-adequate substitute in a household where their mother resided but was unable to care for them.

Perhaps it is easier to blame me than to hold my mother responsible.

Shared DNA
shared history shared memories shared experience
nature and nurture theoretically the same
All painful reminders.

I will always
mourn my siblings.
We didn't have a chance.

CHAPTER FORTY

I am seventeen years old. I have been working after school and on weekends for nearly two years. I need to save money to move out of my house when I turn eighteen. Working is also an excellent and legitimate means of being away from home.

I am working two different jobs, which I juggle with my last year of high school, preparing for the college entrance examination, a leadership position on the student council, various extra-curricular school activities, and my many chores at home. One job is working at a Levi's shop in one of the small neighboring towns, but on this particular night I am working as a waitress in the town shopping mall. I have been at school all day, worked all evening, and have school tomorrow. It is nearly 10:00 pm by the time I pull into our driveway, planning in my head what homework I will need to finish tonight before I go to sleep.

The house is unexpectedly dark and silent. Something is wrong. My father, like me, is a night owl and always stays up late, and my sister Joan always waits up for me, the light in our room a welcome beacon for me as I round the corner and pull into the driveway. I am apprehensive as I open the door. I turn on the light and see that the kitchen is destroyed: the table is on its side, chairs are turned over, there is broken glass everywhere, wall hangings have been flung around, cutlery and broken plates litter the floor.

I hear myself gasp. Horrified, I ask the thick silence, *what happened*?

My youngest sister, nine-year-old Sue, runs to me from her bedroom. She throws herself into my arms, hysterical and hiccupping from crying. She tells me through her tears that my parents and Joan had an argument ending in a physical fight. My parents wrestled Joan into the car and drove her to the mental hospital, leaving the two youngest girls behind and alone in the silent, broken house.

I am shocked. I ask Sue many questions, none of which she can answer. Why did they fight? Did anyone get hurt? When did all this happen? Which hospital have they gone to? Is Joan okay? Where is Rose? Why did they leave you here by yourselves?

I take Sue to her room and tuck her in and sing to her and tell her stories until she falls asleep, my nine-year-old sister suddenly a toddler again. I am comforting her robotically, my mind numb. Twelve-year-old Rose is asleep, mumbling and restless. I go back to the dark living room and sit in the rocking chair. I am exhausted. I know I can no longer go on this way. I have had enough.

My parents finally come home, and from the stillness of that dark room I quietly ask where Joan is. My mother does not answer, does not acknowledge my question, but goes immediately to her room without saying a word. My father, clearly agitated, refuses to tell me, demanding only that I go to bed.

But I have to know where Joan is. I keep asking my dad, quietly, insistently, a broken record of the same three words, "Where is Joan? Where is Joan? Where is Joan?" He refuses to answer. He becomes more and more angry as my broken record continues, demanding in louder tones that I go to bed, telling me that Joan's whereabouts are none of my damn business.

I ignore his demand to go to bed, and tell him finally that I will sit in the chair until he tells me what they have done with my sister. Our allegiances, previously ignored, have been thrown into the middle of the space between us, in stark black and white, unmistakably a line in the sand. I am aligned with Joan; he is aligned with the intruder in our home.

Frustrated, he finally drags me down the hallway to my bedroom floor and shuts the door. I am limp and do not resist, but as soon as he goes into his room and shuts the door I get up and go back out to sit in silence in the rocking chair in the darkness of the sleeping house.

I sit there all night, rocking, still wearing my greasy waitress uniform, my insides slowly breaking into pieces.

I cannot bear the thought of Joan being away by herself in a mental hospital.

I cannot bear the thought of living in this house without her.

I cannot bear the possibility of what else might happen.

I cannot bear, I cannot bear, I cannot bear.

I rock and rock and repeat over and over again, quietly, sadly—enough.

I feel something deep inside me tear open. I am aware that an essential part of myself is draining away from that chasm, but I am powerless to stop it. The anguish and pain is overwhelming and takes my breath away, but I do not cry. I am numb and yet I feel everything in excruciating detail.

I am in the deepest pit of sorrow and hopelessness and loss and suffering and I am here all by myself.

There is no rescue coming for me.

Nobody even knows I am here.

In this way I pass from night to deep night to early morning to dawn. I watch the thick darkness slowly fade away. I am amazed at the rhythm of nature and marvel at its ability to go on as though nothing has happened when everything is so irretrievably broken.

I am so irretrievably broken.

I hear my father get up and get ready to go outside to do the farm chores. He is shocked when he sees me sitting in the rocking chair still wearing my dirty waitress uniform. I see his face darken with anger, but his only words to me as he goes out the door are that I am to tell anyone who asks that Joan won't be going to school for a while because she is sick.

The punctuation mark to that proclamation is the slam of the door.

Rage.
Hurt.

Carefully cloaked
Seething simmering
Brewing bubbling.

Burst.

Erupting exploding
Ferociously furious
Inevitably inescapable.

Wrecking.

Reckoning.

CHAPTER FORTY-ONE

One of the recurring nightmares that I had for many years is an inability to scream when I am confronted with terrible danger. I open my mouth and scream as loudly and forcefully as I can, but nothing comes out, and there I am, unable to do the one thing that would save me.

Helplessness, hopelessness, desperation, fear. Those are the feelings that dominated my childhood, terrible gaping wounds caused by the collateral damage of the mental illness that lived in and ruled over our home. I told no one outside our family. None of us did. It was our most sacred rule. Unlike my dream, I did not open my mouth to scream, though from time to time I managed a little whisper.

When I was in the eighth grade, one of my favorite subjects was English. I loved writing stories. Once for an assignment I wrote a story about a boy who committed suicide. My teacher, a peculiar man with eleven children of his own, took me aside after class. He was concerned not only that this twelve-year-old girl had chosen such a topic, but also my familiarity with the topic, my obvious identi-fication with the boy in the story and the boy's impetus for wanting to end his life while standing at the very cusp of adult possibilities. I still remember how kind he was, how he looked closely at me while I mumbled answers to his questions about how I was feeling, how things were at home, and did I want to end my life?

"Good. Good. No."

I had managed a tiny whisper, but when it came time to speak up to someone who was listening, no sound came out.

But one of us eventually did scream, a scream that was loud and long and courageous. On the heels of that desperate scream, some of our secrets came tumbling out, though in the end it did not matter.

What happened to cause us to disclose our secrets, secrets that bound us together so tightly and caused so much dysfunction?

What happened was inevitable. It was only a matter of when, and how.

Joan and I are Irish twins, a mere thirteen months apart in age. We shared a bedroom, and we always had one another to confide in. Joan could always make me laugh, could always come up with a one-liner to make comical sense out of what was often a ghastly reality. Though we were a year apart in school, we shared friends, and we often socialized together on the weekends. She was not only my sister, but also my closest friend, my confidante, my ally. The most sensitive of all of us, what happened in that house as we grew up weighed most heavily and profoundly on her.

It was Joan who was finally able to scream out loud.

My sixteen-year-old sister finally had the courage to say "enough." Enough of pretending this is normal. Enough of living with an acutely ill parent. Enough of being blasted by collateral damage with no help, no acknowledgement. Enough of carrying around heavy secrets.

Enough trying to scream and no noise coming out. Enough, enough, enough.

And I said it that night, too, but quietly, repeatedly, sadly. Enough.

What is most disappointing about what happened as a result of that night is that even when people finally heard those screams, they did nothing. It is one nightmare to open your mouth and not be able to make the sound of a scream. It is another nightmare altogether to scream loudly and clearly in a room full of people who profess to be able to help, only to have everyone act as though they cannot hear you.

My sister snapped that night, and a violent physical confrontation occurred, as so often occurred. She was trundled off to the hospital mental ward, where she was finally able to give voice to the nightmare we lived. She was a good patient and listened to those mental health professionals carefully. They did not provide her with the same courtesy.

Was it easier for them to treat the patient than the family? Were they not trained to look at the situation holistically? Did any of that team have the slightest curiosity about the conflicting stories, the reasons behind the clearly troubled sixteen-year-old who voluntarily admitted herself to a mental health unit and lived away from her family for six weeks over the Christmas holidays?

Joan told the psychiatrist exactly what was happening in our house. He organized a family meeting, which was preceded by smaller meetings with individual members of our family with individual psychologists. The psychiatrist organized us into units, with Joan and I one unit; my brother one unit; my two youngest sisters a unit; and my parents a unit. They met with us separately, and I still recall the initial horror I felt when the psychologist who met with us started listing off the litany of abuse and bizarre behavior of my mother as reported by Joan. He was reading from notes written in a file folder he had in front of him with my sister's name on it. I felt sick that this man, this stranger, knew our secrets. Not only did he know them, he had written them down! I remember Joan telling me not to worry, that I could tell this man everything, that he believed us and would help us.

One of the questions he asked us was if we could choose one person to leave the family, who would we choose and why. I was very afraid our responses would get back to my mother, and told him so. He assured me that what we spoke about was confidential, and after some prodding by him and reassurance by Joan, I confirmed what Joan had told him about our mother. I was relieved to finally name that I wanted my mother to leave the house, to leave us alone, to allow us some peace, to stop abusing and degrading us. What a comfort to me to describe, finally, the collateral effects of my mother's mental illness to this mental health professional, lay it all in this man's capable hands to fix. As he scribbled his notes, I remember still how hopeful I felt that things would finally change.

After our individual caucuses, we met as a group, the whole family and the psychologists "assigned" to our individual groups. Incredibly, the psychiatrist asked us that same question in our full assembly: if we could get rid of one member of our family, who would it be? None of us dared say that we would choose to get rid of our mother. His repeated questions about which family member was the cause of the problems in the household were met with thick, stony silence.

This was dutifully noted in Joan's file folder.

We had to go home with the one who was the cause of the problems. We knew better. So we all stared at the floor and said nothing.

And then we left Joan there for more "treatment," and the rest of us drove home together.

That was the end of our "family counseling."

So much for screaming.

I wonder whether they wrote "CURED" on Joan's file folder?

Riddle me this:
If a child screams for help
in a room full of people
whose job
(for which they have been educated and trained)
is to hear her and help her
but they do not help her
Did she make a noise?
The answer is this:
Apparently not.

CHAPTER FORTY-TWO

When I was seventeen years old I became physically ill. I found it difficult to eat, as eating caused a burning in my stomach. If I did not eat, I still had the burning sensation in my stomach. I was frequently tired, but found it difficult to sleep. I felt nauseated most of the time. I was in that well of hopelessness I knew so well, and I could barely see light at the top. I felt like crap.

This illness came on the heels of the biggest crisis our family had faced—we were "outed." Our secrets had become known—some of them anyway. The craziness that went on in our house became words on paper, notes made by various psychologists and a psychiatrist charged with fixing what was wrong with us. Like Humpty Dumpty, it seemed our family had finally fallen off the wall and shattered. And like the king's horses and the king's men, the psychologists and psychiatrist couldn't put us back together again.

People at school knew, too. We were instructed to lie and say that Joan was ill, and nothing more. Secrets still had to be maintained, after all. But it was clear that something was seriously wrong with our family. So used to seeing Joan and me together at school, many of the teachers went out of their way to ask me about her, and when she would be returning. Our friends, too, knew that something was wrong, but I couldn't tell them the truth.

The stress was incredible for me. Joan signed herself into the mental hospital, so she was able to choose who visited her. She was there over Christmas and well into the new year, and I was the only family member she allowed to visit her. I spent as much time as I could there, though my parents forbade me to see her, so I had to sneak to do so. It was the first year I spent Christmas without her, and Christmas, never a merry time in our house, was especially glum and dreary that year.

I visited Joan regularly during those many weeks she was in the hospital, and I noticed something that shook me and caused my slide into darkness to become significantly more serious: because Joan was told, day after day, that she had problems, eventually she developed the very problems that they told her she had. What was troubling was that Joan started to demonstrate symptoms of problems she did not have prior to admitting herself to the hospital. She developed problems she did not have prior to the "family counseling" session orchestrated by the mental health professionals. I could feel my sister slipping away from me, slipping away from who she was, and I was helpless to do anything about it. And I couldn't tell a soul.

After several weeks of my own illness and a noticeable weight loss, my father took me to our family doctor. That in itself was amazing. My dad's remedy for any ailment was to take an aspirin and get some sleep.

I had known my doctor all my life. He had delivered all my mother's babies, treated us for our various childhood ailments and injuries, and knew us well. He was also my mother's primary doctor. He asked me several questions, did a few tests, and cheerfully announced that I had an ulcer.

He leaned in toward me, chuckling, and asked me what in the world a girl like me was worrying about to cause an ulcer. What was significant was that he did not expect me to answer. It was a rhetorical question.

I remember thinking clearly, in very teenage fashion, that he was an idiot.

Here was a man who had to have had some idea of what was happening in our home. He was our family doctor. He knew the medical history of everyone in my household, including my mother. That a seventeen-year-old girl from that household was presenting with an ulcer had to have been amazing and telling in its own right. I suppose it was easier for him to believe that I was stressed out about which shoes to wear with my prom dress rather than whether the secrets I was forced to keep were having an effect on my body, or whether I would survive another night of my mother's frightening wandering, or whether my best friend was ever going to come home, and if she did, whether I would even know her anymore.

He either had a disturbing lack of imagination or he was an idiot.

It wasn't just the doctor who pretended that nothing was wrong. Joan missed nearly four weeks of school, all on the pretense that she was "sick." I found out later that the school staff knew something was very wrong in our household, but no one knew what to do, and the nearly unanimous staff consensus was that the school should not involve itself in the affairs of our family. Mr. Shrupp was the only faculty member who not only disagreed with that decision, but acted on it, casting out a life line to me when I desperately needed it.

We, of course, were told to maintain our secret at all costs. We knew the penalties for disclosing our secret. My brother was already gone from school and from the household, so it was easy for him to go along with it. My youngest sisters went to a different school than Joan and I, so it was easy for them as well.

I had to walk the halls without her, had to lie about her supposed illness day after day, had to pretend that nothing was wrong when I felt like my whole world was spinning out of control and literally everything was wrong. People at school were naturally curious about why she was so sick, why she was missing so much school, when she was going to come back. They wanted to talk about it. I knew I could not.

One class Joan and I had together was band, and every day the band instructor asked me in front of the entire class where my sidekick was. Every day I woodenly replied that she was sick. One day, ten minutes after this exchange, I was amazed to feel wetness in my eyes and on my cheeks, and I realized that I was crying without being consciously aware of it. I felt completely hollow inside, yet my heart and my eyes continued to function, continued to feel and emote. I have great respect for this part of me that held me together, allowed me to simply leave what was too overwhelming for me while allowing my physical body to process what it could.

Looking back on that time period of my life I know now that I simply checked out, removing myself from my body, from my reality, from the agony that was my life. I had no other choice. We had already screamed for help, and nobody listened.

I hope that they didn't really hear us.

It's easier than believing that they didn't care.

Too much pretending
Too much to carry
Made my heart leak out my eyes
And I did not even realize it.

CHAPTER FORTY-THREE

It was always easy for me to blame my mother for what happened in my childhood home.

But a big part of this story necessarily involves the other adult in that home. My relationship with my father has been the most complex relationship of my life. It has been one of the most devastating and, ultimately, the most rewarding. I have great respect for my dad, who was a wonderful grandfather to my children and who, in the final years of his life, did his utmost to try to make amends to his children for their childhood. Doing so took great courage, and I am proud to be the daughter of a man who acknowledged his personal shortcomings and worked so hard to be a better person.

My dad was always both a mother and a father to me. I adored him, and when he was in the house things were often better. The problem is that he was rarely in the house. My dad tried to avoid the storms of my mother at all costs, even to the point of enduring her verbal tirades and agreeing to her paranoid accusations and encouraging us to do the same.

He knew what was happening but chose to do nothing.

He did not keep his children safe from his wife.

He did not protect me.

I could not face these truths. As a child and adolescent I absolved him from any blame. He was my final parent. Losing him to my anger and his culpability would have made me an orphan, so I chose instead to make excuses for the part he played in my dysfunctional childhood home.

But when I was a young adult things changed. My dad's brother died, and our family was torn apart by a fight over my uncle's estate. My dad and I were on opposite sides of a family-wide legal dispute over what many of us thought my uncle intended and what others, including my dad, thought was fair. I was shocked that my dad and I were poles apart. The dispute, which was really grounded in old issues involving my father's family that none of us knew about or understood, turned my wise and funny father into an unreasonable and malicious man I did not recognize.

This divide between me and my dad provided me with the space to view him differently, and, coupled with an intense period of self-introspection, gave me the platform for the resulting epiphany: my dad was as much as, or more, to blame for what had happened to me as my mother.

I was shattered.

Adding to the complexity of that time period was the fact that my dad refused to see me or speak to me, due both to the unfolding estate drama and my mother's demand that he have nothing to do with me. We had no contact at all with each other for several years.

I lost my only real parent and all my siblings. I was adrift and alone and often struggled to find an incentive to do well. Many times I could not see the point. I had no one with whom to celebrate my successes, share my worries, talk about my insecurities, my dreams, my plans. I made few lasting, meaningful connections with people. I studied in Europe and travelled on a shoestring, living on part-time jobs and academic scholarships. When I did come to my hometown, my family consisted of my Gram, my Aunt Veronica and my cousin Joe. I never saw my parents and rarely saw my siblings.

As painful as those years were, they provided me with the benefit of stepping completely back and away from my family and provided me with healthy perspective—the first of my life. That perspective helped me to become very self-motivated, largely because I knew it was up to me—and only me—to make my life better. I consciously made the decision that the first eighteen years of my life were not going to ruin the rest of my life.

It was my return to the Midwest that helped to provide me with direction in my life. One of the few good friends I made while attending university encouraged me to go to law school and continued to cheer me on. An old high school friend agreed to be my roommate. These two lifelines were instrumental to me finding meaning, purpose—and peace—in my life.

It was during this time period that something significant happened: I heard from my dad for the first time in many years. He called to tell me that his wife of thirty years had packed up a U-Haul and left a note to say she was leaving him.

He was devastated.

But my mother's leaving allowed my dad to gain a healthy perspective, too. During the last twenty-five years of my father's life he worked hard to become the father and the man that collateral damage had denied him.

My mother's leaving allowed my dad and me to go past the hurt to understand why he responded—or did not respond—as he did. It also provided my dad with insight into me and the manifestations of the collateral damage of my childhood. It allowed us to work through many of the issues of my childhood, which provided us both with peace.

My dad recently passed away. The shock and finality of losing the person who had been both parents to me caused me to stumble, numb, through a haze of loss and grief. Once again I felt adrift and alone.

My mother came to his wake and stopped in front of me in the receiving line. This small woman, whom I look so alike, but from whom I am so very different, was nervous. So was I. I could feel my siblings all looking at us, worried about the exchange. She held one of my hands and said with sincerity, "I am so sorry Cate. I know how close you were to your Dad."

It was the nicest thing she has ever said to me.

I thanked her, the moment passed, and she continued down the receiving line.

What I should have added was this: "Thank you for giving me back my Dad."

He didn't always get it right
Who does?
But we sorted it out
And when the old issues flared
We sorted it out again.
(The really big stuff needs a tune-up periodically)

My dad had courage.
He had the courage to look at himself
And the courage to try to change what wasn't working.
The courage to admit he might not have done it right.
The courage to face the rage of his children
The courage to admit that at times he lacked courage.

CHAPTER FORTY-FOUR

Looking back now I can identify the "what ifs" that would have resulted in a much different childhood.

What if my mother had gotten appropriate and ongoing treatment?

What if there wasn't such stigma attached to mental illness, so that we could have had some support from professionals and the community?

What if it was acknowledged by health professionals, educators and others that parental mental illness has discrete, damaging effects on children and those discrete, damaging effects can not only be identified, but addressed?

Those things did not happen. I was a little girl, disenfranchised and dependent upon the adults around me. It is my right to say now with the relative wisdom of adulthood: what happened when I was a child was not my fault. And it is best to say it with my adult arms securely and lovingly wrapped around that little girl.

"It's all right," it is my responsibility to tell her gently.

"You did the best you could."

"You were a child. "

"It was not your fault."

These powerful sentences chip away at the very core of the false truth of my childhood, the default setting I have carried through my life—I thought my childhood was my fault.

I have come to realize with a sinking feeling and sense of dismay that the wounds I carry from my childhood will need attention for the rest of my life. While I rejoice when I identify and confront an issue, and celebrate when I break one of my old patterns, I know that eventually another of the many hurts from my childhood will manifest. I know that each time that occurs I have the choice of either moving forward toward my potential, painfully facing yet again the collateral damage caused by mental illness living in my childhood home, or throwing up my hands in despair.

It is exhausting. It can be discouraging. Often it is painful. Sometimes it feels as though I have taken one step forward and two steps back.

It was not just my mother living in that house with a mental illness. We were all living with that mental illness, seven people who were all enormously affected by the lack of available treatment, the stigma, the lack of understanding.

Bombarded by collateral damage.

The kind of damage that occurs to a child with a mentally ill parent is more akin to a chronic, potentially life-threatening disease than an acute injury; it is more like cancer than a broken leg. Treatment of the damage must take this into account.

We are all connected, one to another. We are, all of us, responsible for one another, particularly those who are vulnerable and powerless.

It is my sincere hope that we, as a society, reach out our collective hand to assist and support those who live with mental illness—not just the person with the mental illness, but also that person's loved ones, particularly children. I urge us, as a society, to address the collateral damage caused by mental illness.

Masks

I watch us
a sea of human beings
hurrying here and there
And I wonder:
are we Lilliputians
to someone up there?

And I don't know
if I want the answer
to be
yes
or
no.

But I like to think about it.

Here is a proposal to ponder profoundly
(which means 'to contemplate, muse on, chew over, think
about')
What if we could see beyond
the masks we all wear
to hide our pain, our wounding,
our childishness, our fears
our depth, our dreams
our badness
even our joy and our light...

how would we treat one other?

If we could swim effortlessly beneath the smooth surface of
superficiality-
(which means 'triviality, insignificance, hollowness')
able to see everything

understand how it all fits
how one thing flows to, from and with another
to form this perfect person
and that one
and that one too
our individual intricacies utterly interesting...

Would we?

Do these disguises defend us from what we worry is a pitiless
planet
(which means 'cruel, callous, harsh, unkind')
Concealing our softness, our vulnerability, our dreams
Our suffering, our yearning
So that we can navigate our way safely
Forgetting that we are
Spiritual beings together in this beautiful place
Kindness, compassion, care and concern
as instinctive as our breath...

Or from our own fear of being judged?

Here's what I think, having contemplated this at length
(which means 'I think it about it way too much')
Sometimes we need our mask
to keep us soft in a hard world
and hold precious our unique treasures.
And sometimes we use our mask
because we are afraid
of the possibility of the judgment of others.
It's not always easy to tell the difference...

I don't know for sure.
But I like to think about it.

POSTSCRIPT

I called my mother and invited her to breakfast recently. She is old and alone.

I wanted her to know that I forgive her, that I have come to understand how difficult her life has been, that she did the best she could, that I wish her nothing but the best.

But as I was nervously driving to meet her, after laboring over what to wear, how to look, what I would talk about, and rehearsing in my mind what I would say to her, I realized something extraordinary.

I was going to this breakfast hoping that my mother would decide now that she loves me. I was still trying to gain her approval, all these years later. The conversations I was playing out in my head were not to wish her well but to gain her approval for the person I am.

I pulled the car over and gave thanks that I realized before I met with her how my mindset, my reason for the breakfast invitation, had changed so markedly, how it had become about me rather than about her.

I had breakfast with her, this stranger who gave me half my DNA, who carried me inside of herself and birthed me into this world, this woman who caused me so much fear and pain.

And when, after awkward small talk I told her what I had intended to tell her, my voice so much steadier than my heart, she quietly told me off. Told me that I was mean to her, that I hurt her feelings, that I caused her nothing but trouble, that I was a bad daughter. The monologue of my inadequacy went on for a few minutes, but thirty seconds into it I was able to see it clearly for what it was and sat quietly while she worked her way up that mountain of hurt and back down again.

She finished by saying, "I don't even know you!"

I nodded and apologized, and told her I understood her hurt and that I do not know her either.

I wanted to clarify. "I haven't really seen you for more than thirty years. Are you talking about all these things that happened when I was a child?".

"Yes! That's exactly when I am talking about!" she proclaimed triumphantly.

And then she sat back, satisfied, the absence of any logic or connection in this answer irrelevant to her.

While my mother's responses to my assurances to her were not what I had hoped for, I realized for the first time ever that her responses were what they were, and they were fine. She will never be able to be the mom I want or deserve. *I am finally okay with that.* Her life is small, and this smallness allows her to deal with her mental illness.

I told her that I forgive her.

I told her that I have come to understand how difficult her life has been.

That I realize that she did the best she could.

That I hold no ill feelings toward her and wish her nothing but the best.

I don't want her to think that her oldest daughter despises her.

I don't want her to think that I have rejected her.

I know how that feels.

We all missed out on the joy of family, the opportunity to grow and flourish together. It was taken away from us by mental illness, not by hatred or spite or intentional cruelty or abuse. How can I blame her for that? I cannot.

All of us have the right to peace.

All of us have capacity for compassion and forgiveness.

INTERVIEW WITH THE AUTHOR

Q: What do you hope to accomplish with this book?

A: I hope to raise awareness about the effects of parental mental illness on children. I have identified some of those discrete effects, which I am familiar with as part of my personal experience.

I also want others who grew up with parental mental illness to not feel so alone and isolated in their childhood. I hope this book resonates with others and provides some understanding about their childhood and its effects on them as an adult, and in that, provides some healing.

I really hope as well that this book provokes discussion, highlights the need for action, spurs interest in research on this topic, and convinces policymakers of the urgent need to address the effects of parental mental illness on children.

Q: What advice do you have for mental health professionals when dealing with parental mental illness?

A: What happened to our family when we finally had professional mental health intervention was a disaster. I don't know if mental health professionals always think about these interventions from the perspective of the child. It is obvious in our case that they either did not think of it or dismissed it. I believe these types of ill-conceived interventions still happen.

My advice to mental health professionals dealing with parental mental illness is to treat the family holistically. It is not just the parent with the mental illness that is affected by that mental illness; it is the entire family. Ignoring this reality disregards the collateral damage that occurs to the other members of that family, and sets those children up for their own mental health and other issues. This really is an example of good preventative mental health treatment for the rest of the family.

Listen carefully to the parent and the family members. Realize that a child will likely not feel comfortable honestly discussing their parent in front of the parent. Ask the child—away from their parent—how they can be better supported in that situation. Understand the lack of power the child has in that situation.

Address the obvious effects, such as the child's feeling of being responsible for the parent's mental health, the lack of self-worth by the child, the chaos the child might be experiencing at home, the spill-over effect at school and in life. So that the child does not have to become the adult in the home, practical support for the child in the form of assistance to the parent who is struggling should be sourced, whether through the extended family and friends or through more formal programs.

This is my advice, having lived this reality. We desperately need good research to provide mental health and other professionals with evidence-based ways to better deal with this.

Q: Do you have any suggestions for teachers and educators—or other adults— working with children living with parental mental illness?

A: Some of the lifelines in my childhood were teachers and school personnel, and I'm sure they never realized it and the positive impact they had on me. Children struggling with parental mental illness are small people with very limited power dealing with serious grown up problems the best they are able.

My advice is this: reach out to children who are struggling and let them know that you care. Be a lifeline for that child, whatever that looks like in the situation. It might be reassuring the child that you care and that you recognize their difficulty. Maybe it is assistance with homework. It will depend upon that child's situation. But underpinning it all is this: let that child know that you care, that the child has value, that you recognize and understand that they are having difficulty. Understanding the collateral damage of parental mental health on a child is a critical aspect of understanding how you can help.

Q: As you were writing this book, which reaches back to your childhood some forty years ago, did you have any thoughts about the progress made in mental health treatment over the past four decades?

A: I guess what struck me the most is that we have made very little progress, and while this book is about my childhood all those years ago, it could have been written by a child today, about the treatment of that child's mother today, and the stigma still attaching to it all. That is discouraging, to be honest.

Children are still largely forgotten when a parent is severely mentally ill. Without advocacy to change this, I don't see any real appetite by policymakers to address this.

ACKNOWLEDGEMENTS

So many advocates of mental health work tirelessly and passionately, driven by the most selfless of all reasons—the profound desire to make things better by speaking up for those who have no voice. They often do so with frustrating results, little acknowledgement, and at a steep personal cost—but they never give up. Keith Wilson, Ken Steele, Margaret Cook, Pauline Miles—you are advocates in the truest, purest sense. You inspire me and I have the utmost respect for each of you. Thank you for your wisdom, your feedback and your support.

Margaret and Pauline, you carry this collateral damage, too, and I hope this book provides you with validation and peace.

To my friend Joyce Vidot, who works at the coalface of mental health—thank you for providing your valuable insight and your unwavering encouragement.

To Richard Crane, my writing brother, my cheerleader, my critic—thank you for all that and for making me laugh, too.

We are born to a family and we sometimes choose another. My thanks to my beautiful chosen sisters, Linda Leonard, Lizanne Fernandez, and Ellen Ducrow for providing me with their love and sisterhood.

Many thanks to my fantastic editor and publishing guru, Jean Boles.

And finally, to my daughter, who helped me so much more than she can ever know. Sweetness, you are the most wonderful gift of my life. I am so honored to journey with you.

ABOUT THE AUTHOR

Cate Grace currently divides her time between America's Midwest and Western Australia. She spent fifteen years as a trial lawyer in the United States before moving to Western Australia with her two children in 2004. She has worked in the private sector, the public service and in the non-profit, non-government sector, including public health advocacy.

You may email Cate at:

categrace2@gmail.com

ABOUT THE ARTIST

Stefanie Bennett is a Western Australian based artist specializing in both sketching and oil painting and has exhibited works annually in the Perth Hills. Stefanie completed a Bachelor of Fine Arts in 2012 and is currently spending her time pursuing her dream of becoming an art teacher. Stefanie sees life through the lenses of her travels and her life experiences, and her work reflects that inspiration. Check out more of Stefanie's work via Instagram: stefbennett.art.

Made in the USA
Monee, IL
14 January 2025

76719259R00134